SLAAFGEMAAKT

Rethinking Enslavement in the Dutch Caribbean

SLAAFGEMAAKT

Rethinking Enslavement in the Dutch Caribbean

By Felicia J. Fricke

First published in 2020
as part of the New Directions in the Humanities Book Imprint
http://doi.org/10.18848/978-1-86335-227-7/CGP (Full Book)

Common Ground Research Networks
2001 South First Street, Suite 202
University of Illinois Research Park
Champaign, IL
61820

Copyright © Felicia J. Fricke 2020

All rights reserved. Apart from fair dealing for the purposes of study, research, criticism or review as permitted under the applicable copyright legislation, no part of this book may be reproduced by any process without written permission from the publisher.

Library of Congress Cataloging-in-Publication Data

Names: Fricke, Felicia, author.
Title: Slaafgemaakt : rethinking enslavement in the Dutch caribbean / [by Felicia Fricke]
Description: Champaign, IL : Common Ground, 2020. | Includes bibliographical references. | Summary: "Slavery is never past in the way that we usually think it is: it is present both materially and psychologically in the lives of descendant communities, and it is an institution that persists internationally. Consequently, it is imperative that we fully understand the impacts and mechanisms of enslavement in the past so that we can help to dismantle them in the present. In recent years, researchers have used archaeological, sociological, and historical data to examine the lives of enslaved people. Using data not only from archaeological, sociological, and historical sources, but also original osteological, archaeological, and oral historical data, the author weaves stories about the lives of enslaved people that are personal and meaningful, and that take into account both the physical and psychological effects of enslavement"-- Provided by publisher.
Identifiers: LCCN 2020036564 (print) | LCCN 2020036565 (ebook) | ISBN 9780949313379 (hardback) | ISBN 9781863352260 (paperback) | ISBN 9781863352277 (adobe pdf)
Subjects: LCSH: Slavery--Caribbean Area. | Slave trade--Caribbean Area.
Classification: LCC HT1071 .F75 2020 (print) | LCC HT1071 (ebook) | DDC 306.3/6209729--dc23
LC record available at https://lccn.loc.gov/2020036564
LC ebook record available at https://lccn.loc.gov/2020036565
Cover Photo Credit: Felicia Fricke; embroidery was done by H. E. Fricke-Hofman.

Table of Contents

Acknowledgements xi

Figures xiii

Chapter 1 1
How to Unravel the Silence:
Rethinking the Study of Caribbean Enslavement
    Introduction
    The Dutch Caribbean: Mild and Tranquil
    Postcoloniality and Reflexivity
    A Qualitative Methodology: Nuance and Understanding
    Conclusion

Chapter 2 13
Curaçao: A Broken Heart
    Bullenpees
    Double Colonisation
    The Kunuku House
    La Virgen Del Valle
    Datu and Kadushi
    Fleur de Marie
    Stainless Steel
    Veeris Plantation

Chapter 3 53
St. Eustatius: A Golden Rock
    A Chinese Garden
    Fort Amsterdam
    Perfume

    Witten Hoek
    The Blue Beads
    A Fish-Hook
    The Tomb of Mr Moore
    The Lazaretto

Chapter 4 85
St. Maarten: A Useless Island?
    Zoutsteeg
    The Slave Walls
    The Water Pot
    Nickernuts
    The Rock Crystals
    Rockland Plantation
    One Tete Lokay

Chapter 5 115
Conclusions
    The Lifeways of Enslaved People in the Dutch Caribbean
    Enslavement Rethought
    Social and Political Impact
    Final Words

Glossary

Index

For Charlotte Sabey-Corkindale

Acknowledgements

The road to the end of a monograph is very long. My thanks are due not only to the people who helped me during my doctoral research (upon which this book is based), but also to those who supported and encouraged me afterwards. Firstly, my academic supervisors, Professor Sophia Labadi, Professor Ellen Swift, and Dr Efrosyni Boutsikas at the University of Kent, were an inspirational team without whom I would not be half the researcher that I am today.

    In the Caribbean, there were many local professionals who kindly took the time to help me: Reese Cook, Sue Sanders, Gay Soetekouw, Dr Ruud Stelten, Pardis Zahedi, Frank van Spelde, and Fred van Keulen at SECAR; Dr Jay Haviser and Christopher Velasquez at SIMARC; Amy Victorina and Claudia Kraan at NAAM; Dr Dominique Bonnissent (Regional Curator of Archaeology of Guadeloupe, Saint-Barthélemy and Saint-Martin); Christophe Henocq (Collectivité de Saint-Martin); Misha Spanner (St Eustatius Historical Foundation Museum); Elsje Bosch (St Maarten History Museum); Arend-Jan Speetjens (Soualiga Engineering); Jeanne Henriquez (Kas di Pal'i Maishi); Dr Rose Mary Allen (University of Curaçao); Walter Hellebrand (St Eustatius Monuments Office); Dr Johan Stapel (Caribbean Netherlands Science Institute); Lisa Davis Burnett (formerly of the St Maarten Daily Herald); Mavis Albertina (Nos Pais Television); and Mark Yokoyama, Jenn Yerkes, and William Allanic at Les Fruits de Mer. Thanks are also due to Dr Jason Laffoon, Dr Andrea Waters-Rist, Dr Sarah Schrader, Dr Rachel Schats, Dr Corinne Hofman, Dr Menno Hoogland, Dr Mike Field, and Dr Karwan Fatah-Black at Leiden University; Dr Michael Rivera (The Arch and Anth Podcast); Dr Matthew Reilly (City College of New York), who introduced me to contemporary archaeology; Dr William Pettigrew (University of Kent), who warned me that I was going to upset a lot of people, and he was right; Dr Christ Deter (University of Kent) for trusting me with her osteological equipment; Dr Niall Finneran (University of Winchester); Dr Whitney Battle-Baptiste (University of Massachusetts Amherst); Karin de Wijs (Dutch Language School); Nathifa Martina (Palabricks); Kerry Dixon (Common Ground Research Networks); the UK Society for Latin American Studies; the University of Kent Centre for Heritage; the Stichting ter Financiering van Barge's Anthropologica; Pepijn van der Linden, who helped make my maps; Amanda Clarke (University of Reading) and Natalie Anderson (formerly of Oxford Archaeology) who taught me to dig when I was 16; and the woman who shouted "AMEN!" during one of my conference presentations.

    I am also very lucky to have an amazing support network of people who are always there when I need them. Some of them have already been mentioned above, but also very important are: Camilla Prince; Alice Haigh and Justin Leslie; Joe, Rosie, Maggie, and Steve Couling; Violet Brand; Dr Emma Slayton; Philippa Jorissen; Dr

Hendrikje Jorissen; Leo and Tiny Fricke; Aro Fricke and Ingeborg Donia; Caroline Collins Kealy; Dr Jessica Palmer; Dr Barbara Veselka; Emma de Mooij; Femke Reidsma; Dr Esther Plomp; Dr Becky Gilmour; Marcel Hennevelt; Matt Davies; Terence Eder; Dr Jimmy Mans; Remco Huijser; Agnes Boomsma; my colleagues at Aspire Style (Oxford) and The Bishop (Leiden); and my parents, Harm-Jan Fricke and Kathryn Bramble, for whose help and encouragement (not only during this research, but throughout my life) I am extremely grateful.

Lastly, I would like to thank my interviewees. The way you welcomed me reminded me how amazing human beings are, and the things you said about slavery will stay with me forever.

Figures

1.1 Map of the Caribbean showing locations of the three islands addressed in this study: St Eustatius, St Maarten/St Martin, and Curaçao

2.1 Map of Curaçao showing locations of key sites: Plantation Knip, the Kas di Pal'i Maishi museum, Veeris Plantation, and Willemstad

2.2 A rod (bullenpees) made from a bull's penis, curated at the Kas di Pal'i Maishi museum

2.3 The skull of a young woman buried in Pietermaai, Willemstad, during the 18th or early 19th century

2.4 Traditional kunuku house at the Kas di Pal'i Maishi museum

2.5 Candle holder from the Kenepa/Knip village showing the Virgin Mary (La Virgen del Valle

2.6 View of the plantation house at Knip

2.7 Early 20th century map of Willemstad and neighbourhood of Scharloo

2.8 Worn stainless steel knife from the Kenepa/Knip village

2.9 Skull of a man buried at Veeris Plantation in the late 19th or early 20th century

3.1 Map of St Eustatius showing key sites: Scotsenhoek Plantation, Fair Play Plantation, Witten Hoek, the Lazaretto, Fort Amsterdam, and Oranjestad

3.2 Fragment of Delftware found at Fair Play Plantation

3.3 The skull of a woman buried at Fort Amsterdam in the 18th century

3.4 Glass perfume bottle stopper from the Fair Play Plantation enslaved village

3.5 Pewter spoon and iron alloy object (possibly a a bosun's whistle) found in a burial at Witten Hoek

3.6 Five-sided blue glass replica bead by Jo Bean (left) and blue glass marble bead from Ghana(right)

3.7 Iron alloy fish-hook found in the Schotsenhoek Plantation enslaved village

3.8 The tomb of Mr Moore in Old Church Cemetery, with the Quill volcano in the background

3.9 The ruins of the Lazaretto (leprosarium), which operated from the late 19th to the early 20th century

4.0 Map of St Maarten/St Martin, showing sites on the South/Dutch side (Rockland Plantation, Golden Rock Plantation, and Philipsburg) and the North/French side (Mont Vernon and Marigot

4.1 Upper jaw of a man buried at Zoutsteeg, Philipsburg, in the late 17th century

4.2 Drystone walls ('slave walls') at Rockland Plantation during development by Rainforest Adventures

4.3 Traditional ceramic pot for keeping water cool

4.4 Assortment of colourful nickernuts used for playing games

4.5 Quartz crystals from the enslaved village at Golden Rock Plantation

4.6 The upper front teeth of a woman buried at Rockland Plantation during the late 18th or early 19th century, showing wear to the enamel on the inside surface

4.7 Artist's impression of the statue of One Tete Lokay which used to stand on the Little Bay roundabout, to the west of Philipsburg

CHAPTER 1

How to Unravel the Silence: Rethinking the Study of Caribbean Enslavement

INTRODUCTION

This book is intended as a wake-up call. Slavery is a sensitive social and political topic, and many people therefore avoid talking about it in both public and private life. This is for many reasons: those whose families were forcibly transported across the Atlantic Ocean and worked to death in the Americas may be unwilling to discuss a topic that is so personally painful, while the descendants of white Europeans who profited from the slave trade may encounter feelings of guilt or anger when confronted with the crimes of their ancestors. Additionally, there is a layer of discomfort associated with conversations about racism and discrimination that has the potential to silence important discussions before they become useful (Mullins 2010, 375-385). A good example of this happened to me during a presentation that I gave explaining what I was planning to do for my Master's thesis (which was about people of African ancestry in post-medieval London). I finished the presentation and waited expectantly for someone to provide helpful comments. The only faculty member in the room, who was a white woman, could only bring herself to comment, "But are you allowed to call them Black?" There was no discussion of the importance of the research questions or the effectiveness of the research methodology. This white woman could only focus on how uncomfortable any mention of race made her feel. Potential avenues of research in many disciplines have been aborted at this point because white people are still dealing with their guilt.

In 2003, Iyer et al. from the University of California, Santa Cruz, published an article entitled *White guilt and racial compensation*. The article was intended to explore the effectiveness of white guilt as an indicator of support for social equality schemes. They explained how guilt is a 'self-focussed' emotion and does not therefore necessarily translate into beliefs that support equality. By contrast, the authors found sympathy to be an 'other-focussed' emotion which had a better relationship with support for affirmative action policies in the US (Iyer, Leach, and Crosby 2003, 117-129). I took one very important point away from this article: guilt is selfish, but sympathy is productive. With that in mind, I invite you to keep reading.

***

Historians have been studying slavery in the Caribbean for many years, and (as is often the case in academia) the field is still dominated by living white men analysing the words of dead white men. Of course, one wonders whether the dead white men were really qualified to comment on the life experiences of enslaved people in the first place. They had many reasons (both conscious and unconscious) for painting a rosy picture of enslavement, and indeed many of them did. Slave owners often imagined that they enjoyed a paternalistic and reciprocal relationship with the people they had enslaved (Walvin 2013: 147). Unfortunately, historians and other scholars have often failed in a deconstruction of the attitudes of contemporary writers who believed these necessary lies and have not therefore arrived at narratives which foreground the enslaved person. In my opinion, this failure is due to two main phenomena: first, that scholars (especially white male historians, of whom there are many) have inadequately considered the effect that their own privileged identities have on the interpretations that they make (this is called hermeneutics and is very important in archaeology, as I will discuss later); and second, that studies of slavery have often neglected to address the psychological aspects of enslavement and have instead chosen to focus on economic and administrative aspects which may in reality have had little effect on how enslaved people lived their lives. Certainly, they do not help us get closer to the personal stories of those who were enslaved. So, how can we approach the study of slavery in a way that takes both of these problems into account, and makes a concerted effort to solve them?

THE DUTCH CARIBBEAN: MILD AND TRANQUIL

Firstly, it is important to identify a field of study in which to rectify these two scholarly problems. It would have been possible to choose almost any area of the Caribbean, but I chose three islands in the Dutch Caribbean: Curaçao, St Eustatius (also known as Statia), and St Maarten. This was because they represented good targets for interdisciplinary study which were diverse, but which could also be easily compared as they shared (and share) a colonial oppressor.

Geographically, the Dutch Caribbean islands are separated into two groups. Aruba, Bonaire and Curaçao form the Leeward Islands, lying in a line off the coast of Venezuela. Curaçao is the largest island, with Aruba to its west and Bonaire to its east. The Windward Islands, consisting of St Maarten (half of which is actually French and instead referred to as St Martin), St Eustatius, and Saba, lie in a rough triangle to the northeast, on the other side of the Caribbean Sea (Haviser 2001, 60-81).

From 1954 until 1986, these six islands formed an overseas protectorate of the Netherlands called the Netherlands Antilles (Oostindie 1992, 103-119). In 1986, Aruba became autonomously governing within the Kingdom of the Netherlands, followed by St Maarten and Curaçao also becoming autonomously governing in 2010. Bonaire, Saba, and St Eustatius now have a much closer political and organisational relationship with the Netherlands and operate as overseas municipalities (Ministerie van BZK 2019). This has resulted in some communities feeling that they are being

How to Unravel the Silence: Rethinking the Study of Caribbean Enslavement

'recolonised' as the Kingdom of the Netherlands takes on a bigger role in finance and governance (Roitman 2013).

Figure 1.1: Map of the Caribbean showing locations of the three islands addressed in this study: St Eustatius, St Maarten/St Martin, and Curaçao.

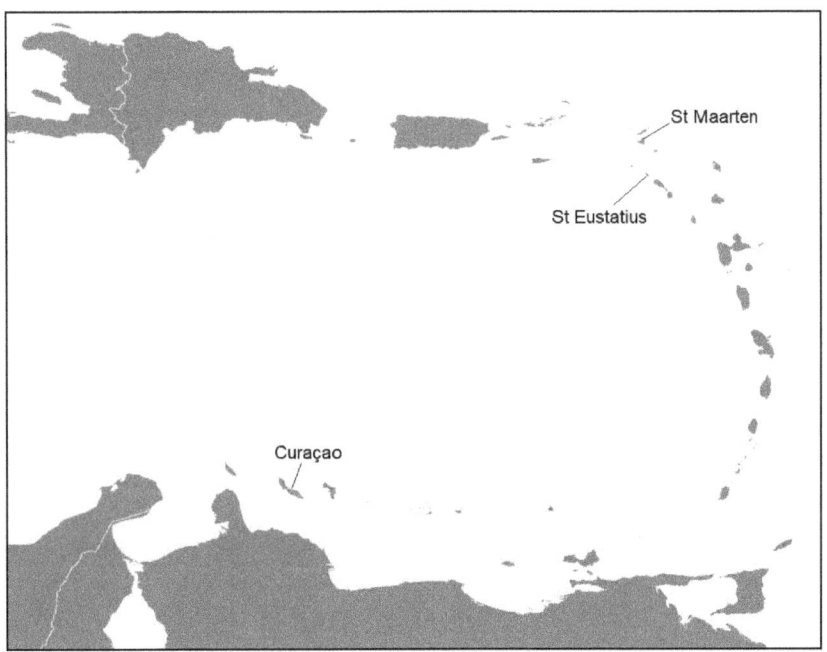

Source: Pepijn van der Linden and Felicia J. Fricke.

Although they all came under Dutch colonial rule, these islands are still geographically, culturally, and politically diverse. This is partly because the Dutch had little linguistic, cultural, or religious impact in their colonies in comparison to other European states (Oostindie 2005: 127-128). In the Leeward Islands, the main languages spoken are Dutch and Papiamentu (or Papiamento in Aruba), while the Windward Islands are English-speaking. There are also other cultural differences which relate to their location and history, for example differing dominant denominations of Christianity. These islands were also too dry to support the booming plantation economies of larger Caribbean islands. Instead, they were important as trade centres (Curaçao and St Eustatius) and salt producers (Bonaire and St Maarten) (Haviser 2001, 60-81).

The differences in historical and modern development amongst these small islands, and the continuing impact that slavery heritage has upon their living inhabitants, makes them ideal subjects for study and comparison. However, the international scene of slavery studies has mainly concentrated on the English, French, and Spanish islands. Few people learn Dutch or Papiamentu as a foreign language, and this makes local resources inaccessible for many. Scholars in the Netherlands may also be uncomfortable with studying such topics, as they challenge firmly-held beliefs about Dutch society being tolerant, liberal, and innocent (Çankaya and Mepschen 2019; Wekker 2016). The small amount of research that has been conducted here neglects the contributions of African descendants in favour of the European elites (Allen 2015, 94-110). Even historical research purporting to focus on the lives of enslaved people still sometimes falls into the trap of Eurocentrism (see for example Roitman 2017). The Dutch Caribbean is therefore particularly in need of new approaches to the study of slavery because it suffers from precisely those problems outlined at the beginning of this chapter. A selection of relevant examples can be found below.

> "The comparatively subdued and even slightly positive tone of this [written] imagery probably reflected the relatively mild character of Curaçao slavery." (Oostindie 2005: 39)

> "The master-slave relationship in Curaçao could be termed mild, because the commercial character and arid climate of the colony made large slave gangs economically unfeasible; both the distribution of the number of slaves per master and the numerical proportion between masters and slaves was much less dramatic on this island than in the slave colony of Surinam." (Hoetink 1972, 59-83: 79)

> "[St Maarten] did not exhibit the characteristic of harsh treatment of slaves." (Paula 1993: 185)

> "Contemporary observers found Dutch Antillean slavery relatively mild. Most visitors to the Dutch Antilles wrote home that the slaves on the islands behaved much more freely than did their counterparts in Dutch Guiana. Unfortunately, there is little information about the living conditions of the slaves on the Dutch Antilles." (Emmer 2011, 450-475: 467)

These descriptions of mildness and tranquillity have a silencing effect upon the people of the Dutch Caribbean, who are still experiencing the lasting social and political effects of slavery. The development of new narratives is therefore extremely important, not only for the development of local Caribbean identities, but also in terms of a wider understanding of modern slavery and inequality. The next sections will discuss how I approached the development of these narratives, and the data sources that I used.

POSTCOLONIALITY AND REFLEXIVITY

It is important to approach research like this from a strong (and explicit) theoretical standpoint. I chose a *postcolonial* approach, which has often been used to refocus scholarship on marginalised groups such as enslaved people (Ashcroft, Griffiths, and Tiffin 2006: 1-4). It is an area of theory which acknowledges the effects of past (and present) colonialism on modern social, political, and economic environments, including the ways in which modern scholars interpret their data (Stoler 2013, 1-29). A related school of thought is that of *decoloniality*, a project of political and epistemological de-linking from colonialism (Bhambra 2015, 115-121). Given that the two schools of thought share emancipatory agendas, they can be combined in an approach which Gurminder Bhambra calls *connected sociologies* (Bhambra 2015, 115-121). Postcolonial projects often have a decolonial goal: the deconstruction of colonial attitudes in academe, as well as in people's personal and public lives.

Although there are several intersecting areas of postcolonial theory (including hybridity and entanglement, race and diaspora) that are highly relevant to the study of slavery in the Caribbean, the most relevant part of postcolonial theory for the research discussed here is *subaltern studies*. It developed as an interdisciplinary approach to South Asian historiography in the 1980s and has a somewhat complicated history, but the term *subaltern* was originally used by the Marxist theoretician Antonio Gramsci in the 1920s and 1930s to refer to any low-status person or group (Louai 2012, 4-8). For him, subalternity could be related to diverse aspects of personal identity such as class, race, gender, and ethnicity (Prakash 1994, 1475-1490: 1477). In recent years, Black feminists amongst other scholars have sought to address these different identities not separately but as part of a web (see Battle-Baptiste 2011: 29). This is called *intersectionality* and is a cornerstone of fourth-wave feminism (Munro 2013, 22-25). It is very important for postcolonial research because privileging one aspect of identity above others can result in incomplete or biased interpretations (Rajan 2010, 117-138). For example, aspects of identity such as race can have dominant or subaltern meanings dependent on context (Gilroy 2004: 37). Considering the changing functions of identity in different contexts allows the subaltern to retain agency and thereby avoid romantic, essentialised, or noncritical interpretations (Shopes 2014, 257-268).

Gayatri Chakravorty Spivak has since the 1980s been discussing the difficulties of reconstructing subaltern narratives from documentary sources (Spivak 1988, 271-313). However, alternative data sources such as archaeology can provide evidence for subaltern agency that historical documents lack. Indeed, archaeology has in recent years thoroughly engaged with postcolonial approaches by challenging established knowledge about marginalised groups in colonial contexts (Liebmann 2008, 1-20). This operates through asking research questions which foreground the subaltern as well as through engaging with non-western interpretations and schools of thought (Monton-Subias and Hernando 2017, 455-471). However, one should still be careful to bear in mind that the researcher constructs narratives *about* the subaltern, rather than *for* her (James 2016 [2000], 73-91; Schmidt 2014, 445-465). Although the data produced by archaeology are not biased in the same way that historical documents can be, they are biased in different ways and the interpretations of the researcher can certainly be influenced by their own identities and preconceptions. As mentioned above, this is called *hermeneutics* (Shanks and Tilley 1992: 108-111). One way of combatting the hermeneutic effects of one's intersecting identities is through *reflexivity*, which entails the continual re-examination of one's biases and perspectives, and is an intrinsic part of the postcolonial approach (Lydon and Rizvi 2010, 17-33). It increases the usefulness of research because it more fully explains the thought processes of the researcher.

***

In the interests of reflexivity, therefore, I should briefly explain why a white, heterosexual, middle-class, highly educated, British woman should think herself qualified to discuss the lives of enslaved people in the Dutch Caribbean. Although traditional approaches to anthropology perceived an *etic* (outsider) perspective as professional and objective, this had the effect of stifling the voices of marginalised groups (Fontein 2010, 311-322). On the other hand, *emic* (insider) researchers also pose problems, as they must reconcile the goals of academic research with the goals of the community (Roulston 2010, 199-228). In reality, researchers often teeter on the brink between insider and outsider status due to the possession of multiple identities.

I grew up in Oxford and attended a girls' school, after which I went to university at Durham, Bradford, and Kent, where I trained in archaeological sciences and human osteology. My mother is from Manchester, and her parents were a tailor and a schoolteacher. My father was born on Bonaire, one of the six islands of the Dutch Caribbean, but he was educated in Europe. His parents were both Dutch, and his father was a Protestant minister. When they lived on Bonaire, people thought that his mother (my grandmother) was mixed-race. Looking at photographs of her I think that this may well have been true, but it remains a family mystery.

I never visited Bonaire until I was 19, and it was a revelation. There were all sorts of things in my heritage that did not make sense until I saw them in context. My grandmother had done a lot of embroidery of Caribbean scenes, and I had never seen any of the things they depicted in real life before. It was as though something clicked into place. When my father and I arrived on Bonaire, he got in touch with some women who had been in my grandfather's congregation, and they still remembered my father as the blond, brown-skinned little boy who had chased watermelons down the road when the delivery truck took a turn too sharply. The house that my father was born in still stood: orange paint peeling, roof sagging inwards, yard full of weeds, an old refrigerator rusting in the middle of the dusty floor. Connected in these ways to the landscape and history of Bonaire, I felt on some level like I had come home.

I found, returning to the Dutch Caribbean around seven years later, that my Bonairean heritage and other identities (especially as a Brit) had an interesting effect on the way that people reacted to me as a researcher. Quite understandably given the lasting political difficulties between the Dutch Caribbean islands and the Kingdom of the Netherlands, the Dutch have a reasonably bad reputation. Luckily for me therefore, I do not seem Dutch when I speak. Instead, I have a distinctly English accent. I am sure that in other areas of the Caribbean (and the wider world) this would be a disadvantage in terms of generating rapport with stakeholders, but in the Dutch Caribbean it meant that I was not immediately associated with the oppressor. Furthermore, after some conversation with stakeholders they would discover my familial links to Curaçao and Bonaire, be surprised that I knew a few words of Papiamentu, and then very generously welcome me as a Caribbean woman. I must stress that this is not an identity I claim for myself. I speak Dutch much better than I speak Papiamentu, and still after four years of living in the Netherlands it is clear that I will never completely become a Dutch insider, so the same is definitely true of the Dutch Caribbean. But I think that it helped me to engage with my stakeholders in a way that other people perhaps could not have done. I have also found that my vaguely Caribbean identity has given me a strong emotional attachment to the subject that I study. I must therefore tread a delicate line between objectivity and emotion when I do my research. I must also continually address my privileged identities (those of race, class, sexuality, nationality, and level of education) and consider how they interact with my identity as a woman with Caribbean heritage and with the data that I study.

A QUALITATIVE METHODOLOGY: NUANCE AND UNDERSTANDING

Within this postcolonial framework, I decided to use qualitative data to study enslaved people in the Dutch Caribbean. Qualitative data are focused on *meaning* and *personal significance* rather than statistical significance (Braun and Clarke 2013: 4). They allow archaeologists to answer sociological questions concerning issues such as identity and activity, and how these are related to each other (Allison 1999, 1-18: 9). In the context of slavery studies, these types of questions are very important and can help to counteract the abiding historical focus on economy and administration.

However, in order to make strong interpretations that are not Eurocentric or colonial, it is also important to triangulate these data. *Triangulation* is used a lot in qualitative studies to assess the reliability of your results by addressing the same problem from different angles (Braun and Clarke 2013: 285-286). This is something that interdisciplinary scholars do a lot: the narrative becomes stronger the more supporting information it includes. Sometimes the different datasets agree with each other, and sometimes they do not. It is always interesting to discover areas where they do *not* agree with each other, because this has the potential to tell you something about how dominant narratives have been constructed in the past.

Addressing these data at various scales (for example, the local, the national, and the international) is also important in examining cultural complexity (Trouillot 1992, 19-42). The development of rich descriptions at the micro level (for example, one skeleton) can illuminate how individual agency contributes to larger societal developments (the macro level). In the context of missing histories like those of the enslaved, it is very important that the microscale and macroscale talk to one another in this way. It helps us to avoid the automatic ascription of new data to existing dominant narratives (Mimisson and Magnusson 2014, 131-156).

In this study, I use my own original data from human skeletons and archaeological artefacts as the focus for microhistories which relate these small pieces of evidence to the macroscale. These are then supported by oral historical evidence from interviews which I conducted in English and Dutch, as well as information from other authors in the related disciplines of sociology, anthropology, ethnography, medicine, psychology, and traditional history as well as those in archaeology. Each of these original data sources has something unique to contribute.

Archaeology

Studies of material culture can provide an insight into daily activities that were thought too ordinary to be recorded in writing, or of which the ruling classes were unaware (Singleton 2010, 185-198). Archaeological evidence such as domestic structures, palaeobotanical (plant) and zooarchaeological (animal) remains, artefacts, and the distribution of these within sites, can be linked to wider concepts such as identity and inequality, especially when triangulated with other sources of evidence (Singleton 1995, 119-140). In this way archaeology lends itself to the microscale (such as artefact biographies) and the macroscale (such as international trade networks).

Osteology

Human remains represent the most direct evidence for people who lived in the past (Gowland and Knusel 2006, ix-xiii). They can provide information on behaviour, lifestyle, disease, and culture (Schutkowski 2008, 1-11). Here I use the approach of *osteobiography*, which is the study of one individual using multiple sources of information to build a picture of the society in which that person lived (the macroscale), as well as specific details about the life of that individual (the microscale) (Stodder and Palkovich 2012, 1-8). This approach provides us with the personal stories of enslaved people in a way that historical documentation cannot.

Oral History

People may inherit narratives focused around traumatic events, such as enslavement, from previous generations (Jones and Russell 2012, 267-283). Oral history can therefore allow us to access data missing from history and archaeology, such as meaning and emotion. It enables research that is socially engaged and contributes to the democratisation of knowledge by involving multiple participants (Thompson 2016 [1988], 33-39). Oral narratives can provide accurate historical information about the recent past (within 3 or 4 generations) (Boeyens and Hall 2009, 457-481), and qualitative information about people's lives at a distance of around 400 years (Mason 2012, 72-91), which includes the timeframe of Caribbean slavery. The people I interviewed (in 2016 and 2017) were mostly older individuals, because they are chronologically closer to the time-period of slavery, although I did also interview some younger people. The interviewees were also mostly of African or mixed ancestry, although there were also some white people, particularly on St Maarten where there was a majority white population until the 20th century (Rupert 2012: 75). Everyone interviewed had links to the islands through their family, their own experience of living on the islands, or their role as a heritage professional, although often the interviewees possessed two or three of these identities. Throughout this book, oral history interviewees are identified with codes such as CUR-OH-01 to maintain anonymity.

CONCLUSION

This chapter has explained that a postcolonial approach to the archaeology of enslavement in the Dutch Caribbean can be used to address problems with the dominant narrative. Firstly, the use of reflexivity and the multivocal nature of oral history help to combat interpretations that may be colonial, Eurocentric, or both; and secondly, the inclusion of more personal and psychological aspects of enslavement through the use of multiple data sources and a focus on the subaltern can help us to avoid narratives which focus too heavily on economic and organisational aspects of enslaved lifeways. In this way we can get closer to the true stories of those who were enslaved. The following three chapters will use this theory and methodology to explore enslavement on the Dutch Caribbean islands of Curaçao, St Eustatius, and St Maarten: not a comprehensive history of slavery, but one story amongst many.

REFERENCES

Allen, R. 2015. "Toward Reconstituting Caribbean Identity Discourse from within the Dutch Caribbean Island of Curacao." In *Caribbean Reasonings: Freedom, Power and Sovereignty, the Thought of Gordon K Lewis*, edited by Meeks, B. and J. McCalpin, 94-110: Ian Randle Publishers.
Allison, P. 1999. "Introduction." In *The Archaeology of Household Activities*, edited by Allison, P., 1-18. London: Routledge.
Ashcroft, B., G. Griffiths, and H. Tiffin, eds. 2006. *The Post-Colonial Studies Reader*. 2nd ed. London: Routledge.
Battle-Baptiste. 2011.W. *Black Feminist Archaeology*. Walnut Creek, California: Left Coast Press.
Bhambra, G. 2015. "Postcolonial and Decolonial Dialogues." *Postcolonial Studies* 17, no. 2: 115-121.
Boeyens, J. and S. Hall. 2009. "Tlokwa Oral Traditions and the Interface between History and Archaeology at Marothodi." *South African Historical Journal* 61, no. 3: 457-481.
Braun, V. and V. Clarke. 2013. *Successful Qualitative Research: A Practical Guide for Beginners*. London: SAGE.
Çankaya, S. and P. Mepschen. 2019. "Facing racism: discomfort, innocence and the liberal peripheralisation of race in the Netherlands." *Social Anthropology* 27(4): 626-640.
Emmer, P. 2011. "Slavery and the Slave Trade of the Minor Atlantic Powers." In *The Cambridge World History of Slavery, Volume 3: AD 1420-AD 1804*, edited by Eltis, D. and S. Engerman, 450-475. Cambridge: Cambridge University Press.
Fontein, J. 2010. "Commentary: The Efficacy of 'Emic' and 'Etic' in Archaeology and Heritage." In *Handbook of Postcolonial Archaeology*, edited by Lydon, J. and U. Rizvi, 311-322. California: Left Coast Press.
Gilmore III, R. 2005. "The Archaeology of New World Slave Societies: A Comparative Analysis with Particular Reference to St Eustatius, Netherlands Antilles." PhD Thesis., University College London.
Gilroy, P. 2004. *Postcolonial Melancholia*. New York: Columbia University Press.
Gowland, R. and C. Knusel. "Introduction." In *Social Archaeology of Funerary Remains*, edited by Gowland, R. and C. Knusel, ix-xiii. Oxford: Oxbow Books.
Haviser, J. 2006. "Historical Archaeology in the Netherlands Antilles and Aruba." In *Island Lives: Historical Archaeologies of the Caribbean*, edited by Farnsworth, P., 60-81. USA: University of Alabama Press, 2001.
Hoetink, H. 1972. "Surinam and Curacao." In *Neither Slave nor Free: The Freedmen of African Descent in the Slave Societies of the New World*, edited by Cohen, D. and J. Greene, 59-83. London: The Johns Hopkins University Press.
Iyer, A., C. Leach, and F. Crosby. 2003. "White Guilt and Racial Compensation: The Benefits and Limits of Self-Focus." *Personality and Social Psychology Bulletin* 29, no. 1: 117-129.
James, D. 2016 [2000]. "'Listening in the Cold': The Practice of Oral History in an Argentine Working-Class Community." In *The Oral History Reader*, edited by Perks, R. and A. Thomson. 3rd ed., 73-91. London: Routledge.
Jones, S. and L. Russell. 2012. "Archaeology, Memory and Oral Tradition: An Introduction." *International Journal of Historical Archaeology* 16: 267-283.
Liebmann, M. 2008. "Introduction: The Intersections of Archaeology and Postcolonial Studies." In *Archaeology and the Postcolonial Critique*, edited by Liebmann, M. and U. Rizvi, 1-20. Plymouth: AltaMira Press.
Louai, E. 2012. "Retracing the Concept of the Subaltern from Gramsci to Spivak: Historical Developments and New Applications." *African Journal of History and Culture* 4, no. 1: 4-8.

Lydon, J. and U. Rizvi. 2010. "Introduction: Postcolonialism and Archaeology." In *Handbook of Postcolonial Archaeology*, edited by Lydon, J. and U. Rizvi, 17-33. California: Left Coast Press.

Mason, O. 2012. "Memories of Warfare: Archaeology and Oral History in Assessing the Conflict and Alliance Model of Ernest S Burch." *Arctic Anthropology* 49, no. 2: 72-91.

Mimisson, K. and S. Magnusson. 2014. "Singularizing the Past: The History and Archaeology of the Small and Ordinary." *Journal of Social Archaeology* 14, no. 2: 131-156.

Ministerie van BZK. "Waaruit Bestaat Het Koninkrijk Der Nederlanden?" Rijksoverheid. Accessed May 14th, 2019. https://www.rijksoverheid.nl/onderwerpen/caribische-deel-van-het-koninkrijk/vraag-en-antwoord/waaruit-bestaat-het-koninkrijk-der-nederlanden.

Monton-Subias, S. and A. Hernando. 2017. "Modern Colonialism, Eurocentrism and Historical Archaeology: Some Engendered Thoughts." *European Journal of Archaeology* 21, no. 3: 455-471.

Mullins, P. 2010. "Race and Class." In *Handbook of Postcolonial Archaeology*, edited by Lydon, J. and U. Rizvi, 375-385. California: Left Coast Press.

Munro, E. 2013. "Feminism: A Fourth Wave?" *Political Insight* 4, no. 2: 22-25.

Oostindie, G. 1992. "The Dutch Caribbean in the 1990s: Decolonization or Recolonization?" *Caribbean Affairs* 5: 103-119.

———. 2005. *Paradise Overseas: The Dutch Caribbean: Colonialism and its Transatlantics Legacies*. Oxford: Macmillan Caribbean.

Paula, A. 1993. *'Vrije' Slaven: Een Sociaal-Historische Studie Over De Dualistische Slaven-Emancipatie Op Nederlands Sint Maarten 1816-1863*. Zutphen: De Walburg Pers.

Prakash, G. 1994. "Subaltern Studies as Postcolonial Criticism." *The American Historical Review* 99, no. 5: 1475-1490.

Rajan, R. 2010. "Death and the Subaltern." In *Can the Subaltern Speak? Reflections on the History of an Idea*, edited by Morris, R., 117-138. New York: Columbia University Press.

Roitman, J. 2013. *The Dutch Windward Islands: Confronting the Contradictions of Belonging, 1815-2015*. Leiden: KITLV.

Roitman, J. 2017. "'A Mass of Mestiezen, Castiezen, and Mulatten': Contending with Color in the Netherlands Antilles, 1750-1850." *Atlantic Studies* 14 (3): 399-417.

Roulston, K. 2010. "Considering Quality in Qualitative Interviewing." *Qualitative Research* 10, no. 2: 199-228.

Schmidt, P. 2014. "Deconstructing Archaeologies of African Colonialism: Making and Unmaking the Subaltern." In *Rethinking Colonial Pasts through Archaeology*, edited by Ferris, N., R. Harrison and M. Wilcox, 445-465. Oxford: Oxford University Press.

Schutkowski, H. 2008. "Introduction." In *Between Biology and Culture*, edited by Schutkowski, H., 1-11. Cambridge: Cambridge University Press.

Shanks, M. and C. Tilley. 1992. *Re-Constructing Archaeology: Theory and Practice*. London: Routledge.

Shopes, L. 2014. "'Insights and Oversights': Reflections on the Documentary Tradition and the Theoretical Turn in Oral History." *The Oral History Review* 41, no. 2: 257-268.

Singleton, T. 1995. "The Archaeology of Slavery in North America." *Annual Review of Anthropology* 24,: 119-140.

———. 2010. "Slavery, Liberation, and Emancipation: Constructing a Postcolonial Archaeology of the African Diaspora." In *Handbook of Postcolonial Archaeology*, edited by Lydon, J. and U. Rizvi, 185-198. California: Left Coast Press.

Spivak, G. 1988. "Can the Subaltern Speak?" In *Marxism and the Interpretation of Culture*, edited by Nelson, C. and L. Grossberg, 271-313. Urbana, IL: University of Illinois Press.

Stodder, A. and A. Palkovich. 2012. "Osteobiography and Bioarchaeology." In *The Bioarchaeology of Individuals*, edited by Stodder, A. and A. Palkovich, 1-8. USA: University Press of Florida.

Stoler, A. 2013. "'The Rot Remains': From Ruins to Ruination." In *Imperial Debris: On Ruins and Ruination*, edited by Stoler, A., 1-29. London: Duke University Press.

Thompson, P. 2016 [1988]. "The Voice of the Past: Oral History." In *The Oral History Reader*, edited by Perks, R. and A. Thomson. 3rd ed., 33-39. London: Routledge.

Trouillot, M. 1992. "The Caribbean Region: An Open Frontier in Anthropological Theory." *Annual Review of Anthropology* 21: 19-42.

Walvin, J. 2013. *Crossings: Africa, the Americas and the Atlantic Slave Trade*. London: Reaktion Books Ltd.

Wekker, G. 2016. *White Innocence: Paradoxes of Colonialism and Race*. Durham: Duke University Press.

CHAPTER 2

Curaçao: A Broken Heart

Figure 2.1: Map of Curaçao showing locations of key sites: Plantation Knip, the Kas di Pal'i Maishi museum, Veeris Plantation, and Willemstad.

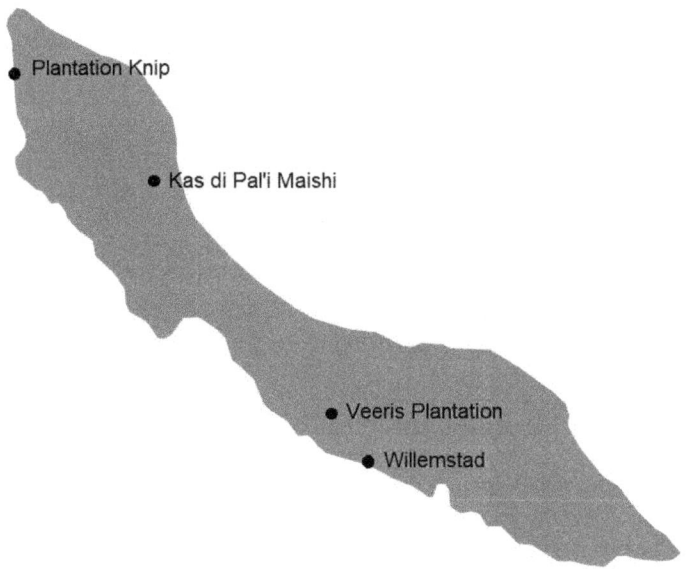

Source: Pepijn van der Linden and Felicia J. Fricke.

BULLENPEES

Figure 2.2: A rod (bullenpees) made from a bull's penis, curated at the Kas di Pal'i Maishi museum.

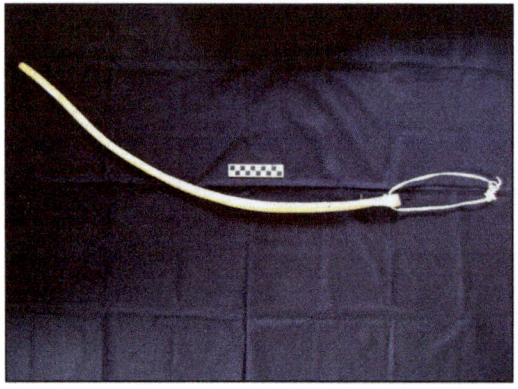

Source: Felicia J. Fricke.

The image above shows a rod made from a stretched, dried bull's penis. In Dutch it is known as a *bullenpees*, but this word is in modern times usually used to refer to dog treats and has therefore lost some of its earlier connotations. The artefact comes from the *Kas di Pal'i Maishi* (House of the Sorghum Stalks), which is a living history museum located in the western part of Curaçao. It consists of a genuine early 20th century traditional house and freestanding oven, which have been restored, and contains hundreds of everyday objects traditionally used by the Afro-Curaçaoan descendants of enslaved people. These include perishable materials (many dating to the mid-20th century, although some are more recent replicas) as well as songs and sayings that are lost in archaeology. The survival of these cultural attributes lends richness and diversity to the evidence for enslaved lifeways in Curaçao.

The *bullenpees* represents a system of punishment that was, for a long period of time, administered by the island government, specifically the *College van Kleine Zaken* or College of Small Affairs for smaller misdemeanours and *de Raad van Civiele en Criminele Justitie* or Council of Civil and Criminal Justice for more serious crimes (Langenfeld 2007, 57). There was supposed to be some control over what slave owners were permitted to do to their enslaved people. Many slave laws, such as those of the French *Code Noir*, encouraged some humanity towards enslaved people, but in practice were roundly ignored (Goveia 1991 [1960], 346-362). A system which operates on fear must operate at all levels in order to maintain itself, and plantation owners across the Americas lived in a state of anxiety over the threat of revolt, which often had fatal consequences for white people. Punishments under the control of the slave owner and under the control of the government could therefore both be extremely harsh. The *bullenpees* is recorded in historical documents as a tool which with the *fitó* (overseer) or *bomba* (slave driver) might beat enslaved people. This was a very serious punishment. The durable and supple surface of the *bullenpees* opened the skin with ease, and could cause such severe injuries that victims might not be able to walk properly for several months afterwards (Brenneker 2018, 14, 16). Historical records also mention beatings with the *watapana* (the branch of a *Libidibia coriaria* or *divi divi* tree) or the bullwhip (Ellis 1981, 21). Even small crimes such as theft, insolence, and fighting were punishable by 75 strokes of the whip or *bullenpees* (Langenfeld 2007, 57).

Those who were thought to require more sustained punishment might be sent to work on the salt pans (Rupert 2012, 142). These were located at Jan Thiel (to the south of Willemstad) amongst other locations, and consisted of shallow ponds full of seawater, which evaporated in the sun. The water became increasingly salty until crystals began to form. When the salt was ready to harvest, the water would turn pink. Enslaved people would then wade into the water, lift out the salt using baskets, and pile it along the shore to dry. Lifting and carrying all day in the hot sun is always very hard work, but these activities are even more difficult in the environment of the salt pan. The white salt reflects light, which can damage your eyesight, while the salt crystals can damage your skin (CUR-OH-09). Mary Prince, who was enslaved on a salt pan on Grand Turk in the Turks and Caicos Islands of the northern Caribbean, described:

> "Our feet and legs, from standing in the salt water for so many hours, soon became full of dreadful boils, which eat down in some cases to the very bone, afflicting the sufferers with great torment." (Prince 2008, 24)

In some cases, extra punishment included deliberately cutting the enslaved person's feet and putting them into the stinging salty water (CUR-OH-10). Despite a reputation for mildness, the physical abuse perpetrated by masters on their enslaved people in Curaçao was no less extreme than in other areas of the Caribbean. Enslaved people who participated in Curaçaoan rebellions might be burnt, dismembered, or broken on the rack (Oostindie 2011, 1-22). Slave owner Willem de Suyder cut through the Achilles tendons of an enslaved man called Martin, because he was a thief (Gibbes, Romer-Kenepa, and Scriwanek 2015, 70). Theft was one area where the opinion of the enslaved person and the opinion of the slave owner were likely to markedly disagree: the owner considered that he deserved to own his property, while the enslaved person was sometimes forced to steal to survive.

Archival materials available at the *Nationaal Archief* in Willemstad also support stories of hard punishments, for example the *Gestrafde Slaven* (Punished Slaves) document which records that an eighteen-year-old girl was punished for running away by being hung from a tree for two days (*Nationaal Archief inventarisnummer 8, arbeid 8*). Documents also record that enslaved people might have their nose or ears cut off, or be burned to death (Langenfeld 2010, 9, 11). One man was dragged around the gallows by his legs, had his hands cut off, and was then killed by a blow to the head with a sledgehammer (Paula 1968, 26). Even pregnant women were not spared. The punishment described is also recorded in St Eustatius and St Maarten:

> CUR-OH-07: when a woman is pregnant and she has to be beaten, [...] they dig a hole, she is going to lie down in the hole, and then they beat her on her back and head.

In order for these punishments to have the greatest psychological effect on the enslaved population, they often took place in public (Gibbes, Romer-Kenepa, and Scriwanek 2015, 70). In Willemstad, the main town of Curaçao, there was an area known as Scavot where enslaved people were punished (CUR-OH-08). It was located in the western part of Willemstad known as Otrobanda (meaning 'other side' in Papiamentu), where many enslaved and free African or African-descendant people lived (Rupert 2012, 3). The punishments therefore happened in a place where they would be observed by the oppressed population. And it worked. Enslaved people were sometimes so afraid of these punishments that they attempted suicide (Langenfeld 2007, 72). This conspicuous violence was necessary in order to transform captives into enslaved people. Indeed, the title of this book comes from the Dutch phrase for enslaved people: *tot slaafgemaakte mensen*. It sounds a little clumsy in Dutch as it does in English, but that is useful: it reminds us that being a slave is not an intrinsic part of your being. Rather, it is something that is done *to* you (Slavernij en Jij 2019).

The anxiety which prompted slave owners to enact these punishments on enslaved people also encouraged them to practice aspects of psychological warfare designed to discourage rebellion (Lewis 1983). For example, the concept of divide and rule was applied to prevent enslaved people forming large united communities, a strong base from which rebellions might be planned. Slave owners and overseers could exploit existing differences (such as field labour vs. domestic labour) within the enslaved population to separate groups from each other:

> CUR-OH-02: and so the manager could be a white person, but there are different *fitós* or managers who were Black people. And in that sense, the aspect of divide and rule, which is from ages, you know, was also used. So you get a person, give him a bit more than the rest, and he thinks he is a king or a queen, you know? And in that sense he or she will do exactly what you want him to do.

They also treated enslaved people as stupid, lazy, childlike, and inferior: this is recorded by the sociologist Orlando Patterson as being a very important part of the process of enslavement, by which the captive person internalises and comes to accept their enslavement (Patterson 1982, 63-64). Remnants of this treatment as a perpetual minor can be observed in the Papiamentu language: the Catholic Church perpetuated the use of the word *yu*, which means child, when addressing Afro-Curaçaoan people well beyond the date of abolition, and the word has even been adopted as part of a wider modern debate on Curaçaoan identity, which discusses who should be seen as a *yu di Kòrsou* (child of Curaçao) and who should not. This discussion is often centred around race (Roe 2016, 92-102).

> CUR-OH-06: when somebody demeans you and speak to you like you're a stupid person, that that hurts also [...] I mean, you make a race hate themselves.

Passivity and lack of confidence are also present in the following story about emancipation at *Landhuis Ascencion* in the western part of the island, where the *bomba* is so afraid of the *shon* (master) that he does not understand the instructions he has been given about emancipation:

> CUR-OH-05: ... the *shon* was, he was not married and he hadn't had children so he called the *bomba*, the one that was actually seeing about the slaves and he gave him all the keys and he told him, tomorrow you will call all the slaves together and tell them that they are free and that they are free to go, and he gives all the keys from every, all those, from the whole *landhuis* and in the morning the *shon* didn't wake up so the *bomba* became nervous, he don't see the *shon*, he don't wake up, so he ran from Dokterstuin to St Willibrordus and get the *shon* from there - the *shon* didn't wake up! And what the *shon* told him to do, to tell the slaves that they are free. So he didn't understand that. He - and the *shon* didn't came out and he has to go and tell them that they are free. So he went and called the *shon* from Willibrordus and they came back to Dokterstuin, to Ascencion, and when the *shon* from Willibrordus break the room open, the *shon* committed suicide. And he collected all the keys from the *bomba* and he became the owner of the *landhuis*. So actually it was given to the *bomba* but he didn't understand that and, you know, he didn't know what was going on, and there was no - actually - real explanation.

Various scholars have noted that slavery in Curaçao (and elsewhere) has had an inherited effect on the modern population similar to Post-Traumatic Stress Disorder (PTSD) (see for example van der Dijs 2011, 135). Associated terms such as Post Traumatic Slave Syndrome (PTSS) and their ability to affect descendant communities are also being discussed by psychologists (Sule et al. 2017, 779-783; Degloma 2009, 105-122). These effects include insecurity about food, insecurity about personal opinion and identity (Marcha and Verweel 2003, 10, 117), internalisation of inferiority, lack of confidence, and shame associated with slavery and African ancestry (CUR-OH-04; CUR-OH-06; CUR-OH-07) as well as a belief that people will not succeed, and mistrust of or anger towards those who do succeed (Paula 1968,

73-74), although this is probably also related to the functions of the Catholic Church after 1863, which purported to offer social advancement through education but really served to control the Afro-Curaçaoan population through adherence to a strict moral code and the valorisation of poverty (Broek 2001, 633-641). This internalisation of inferiority also applies to the way in which the appearance of African-descendant people was (and is) negatively portrayed (see CUR-OH-06 and Allen 2007, 74) and can also be observed in Papiamentu, where an African-descendant individual might be referred to as *hende di tristu kolo* (a person of sad colour) (Paula 1968, 75). There is also a lot of prejudice against *kroeshaar* (Afro hair) and dark skin (Marcha, Verweel, and Werkman 2012) perpetrated within the Afro-Curaçaoan community as well as being received from white people (CUR-OH-02; CUR-OH-06).

These inherited effects are sometimes referred to as 'mental slavery' (Akbar 1996, 16-22), but sociologists have referred to them as *de cultuur van angst* (the culture of fear) (Marcha and Verweel 2003). However, enslaved people also developed coping mechanisms, survival strategies, and modes of resistance which functioned to counteract these psychological effects and helped them recover from physical wounds. The following sections will describe the hardships they encountered as well as how the vibrant and creative Curaçaoan culture developed and thrived under extremely adverse social conditions.

DOUBLE COLONISATION

The following picture shows the face of a young African woman who died during the 18th or 19th century. Today, her burial location is underneath the offices of the *Kamer van Koophandel* (Chamber of Commerce), but while she was alive this area of Curaçao's capital was a wealthy suburb. The Dutch West India Company (WIC) had begun its occupation of the island in Punda, which is still the centre of Willemstad, and this settlement was originally bounded by a wall and surrounded on three sides by water. Gradually, as the population increased, room within the walls became scarce. It became more attractive for successful merchants and landowners to build large houses along the road which led south away from Punda (Rupert 2012, 127-130). This area is called Pietermaai, and many of its crumbling mansions can still be seen today, a string of brightly coloured jewels along the coastline. How did a young African woman come to be buried here?

The biocultural approach exploring the physical effects of life experiences on individuals and populations can be used to answer this question. People do "experience colonial rule in their bodies" (Given 2004, 93). One of the best examples of this type of research is the huge New York African Burial Ground Project, the excavation and analysis of an 18th century population including enslaved people who participated in a rebellion in 1712 (Blakey and Rankin-Hill 2009). Enslaved children in this population experienced delayed development and evidence for frequent episodes of stress during childhood (Goode-Null, Shujaa, and Rankin-Hill 2009, 227-253). There was high infant and adolescent mortality and adults in this population showed skeletal evidence for hard labour fairly evenly between the sexes (Blakey, Rankin-Hill, Goodman et al. 2009, 269-273). We therefore already know that the experiences of enslavement can impact the skeleton, but there is very little research in this area in the Dutch Caribbean.

Figure 2.3: The skull of a young woman buried in Pietermaai, Willemstad, during the 18th or early 19th century.

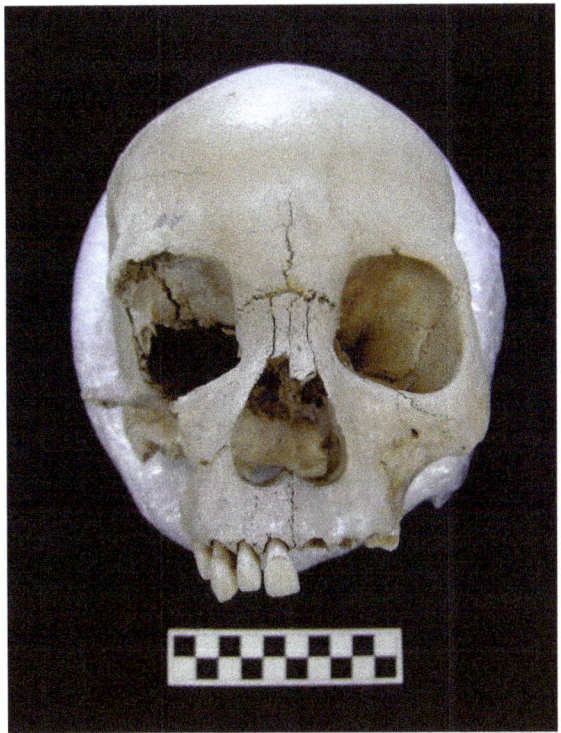

Source: Felicia J. Fricke.

The story of the Kamer van Koophanel individual begins in sub-Saharan Africa. During the 18th and 19th centuries, the WIC, and later on also private investors, were heavily involved in the transatlantic slave trade (Thomas, H. 1997, 255). They had forts at several points along the coast of West Africa (for example Elmina in Ghana), from where they could exchange objects such as beads and cowrie shells for captives held by local traders (Ogundiran 2002, 427-457). Curaçao was one of the most important transhipment points in the Caribbean, providing the French and Spanish with thousands of enslaved people (Thomas, H. 1997: 229). Before sale these people, often unwell after the long sea voyage from Africa, were imprisoned at the Zuurzak and Groot Sint Joris depots on the coast south of Willemstad (Martinus 1997, 4). They were often worked to exhaustion carrying stone or picking salt (Jordaan 2003, 219-257). Healthy people were more likely to sell to foreign buyers, while the old, diseased, and very young were likely to be those who remained behind (Rupert 2012, 82-83). Curaçaoan buyers might purchase these *macquerons* - or enslaved people sold for less money because they were not entirely healthy – hoping that they would recover and then provide profit in resale (Jordaan 2003, 219-257). Indeed, local historians Gibbes et al. (2015) have pointed out that the narrative of 'mild' slavery in Curaçao may refer only to the practise of caring for enslaved people before sale, in the hope of fetching a higher price – a practice clearly disregarded whenever the WIC was suffering from a labour shortage (see Jordaan 2003, 219-257).

Most foreign buyers also preferred men who would be useful on the large sugar plantations for which the Caribbean was famous. This resulted in a sex imbalance opposite to that which prevailed in other areas of the Caribbean (Schiltkamp, Smit, and Wachlin 2000, 21; Thomas, H. 1997, 401). Out of the many women for sale in Willemstad, buyers might select those who could work as domestic servants and prostitutes (Jordaan 2003, 219-257). We can therefore see this young African woman for sale in Willemstad, after a long voyage, possibly sick and therefore not a desirable purchase for foreign buyers. She was probably bought by a wealthy white Protestant or Jewish man and taken to his Pietermaai mansion where the Curaçaoan landscape might be visible to her for the first time: bare rock, hot dust, tall cacti. Pitched against her will into a foreign society, she experienced stress on several levels, not only physically in terms of readjusting to life on solid land and learning the new types of work that she would have to do, but also in psychological terms. She was required to learn a new language and to think of herself as a slave.

It is unclear exactly how old the Kamer van Koophandel individual was when she was forcibly transported to the Americas, but it is likely to have happened in late childhood or early adolescence, according to information from her teeth. Unlike the rest of the skeleton, our teeth do not change and remodel as we get older. They therefore represent a permanent record of some childhood events. By analysing isotopes (types of atoms) of the different periodic elements in dental enamel, which correspond to the types of water and rock in the region where you live, isotopic specialists can work out where you probably spent your childhood (Laffoon et al. 2017). All this is rather approximate: the isotopic results cannot provide a postal address. Instead, they first indicate where in the world you are *not* from. Using the archaeological context of a buried individual, specialists can then narrow the results slightly to work out where you *may* have been from. In the case of this young woman, she certainly did not spend her childhood in Curaçao. Given the archaeological context it is most likely that she spent her childhood in sub-Saharan Africa. This isotopic result corresponds to metric analysis of her skull, which indicates that she was probably of African ancestry (Fricke et al. 2019). I used a forensic computer program called FORDISC 3.0 to do the metric assessment. It compares the measurements you have taken to measurements from a variety of different populations worldwide and tells you which population your individual is most similar to (see Ousley and Jantz 2005).

Our teeth also record other types of information. During childhood or early adolescence, while her wisdom teeth were forming, this young woman underwent a period of profound physical or psychological stress which caused an interruption in enamel production, now seen as a thin horizontal line in the enamel surface (known as *linear enamel hypoplasia* or LEH). In her case, it is possible that this anomaly is actually a record of the Middle Passage itself. However, there are other stressful events recorded on her skeleton which could possibly also have contributed to this interruption. At the left knee joint there is a surface irregularity known as *osteochondritis dissecans*, which develops when part of the joint surface breaks off. It most often occurs during adolescence when an individual engages in high levels of physical activity (Fricke et al. 2019). In modern populations it is frequently observed in individuals who play sports to a high level in their teenage years (Kessler et al. 2014). Even domestic labour was not necessarily light labour and involved an endless round of washing, sewing, and cooking (Langenfeld 2010, 63):

> CUR-OH-06: You probably clean every day, you have to cook every day, you have to [...] bring water every day, you had to dress the people every day, you had to take care of the kids every day [...] it might sound as if it's better [than field work], but maybe they got slapped and hit the whole time in there - you don't know!

Although some historians have classified domestic labour as preferable to plantation labour (see for example Craton 2003 [1997], 103-111), this type of work was likely to bring enslaved people into close contact with their owners (Guerreiro Ramos Bennett 1999, 227-233) and this was not necessarily advantageous:

> CUR-OH-06: the ones in the house were more accessible, you know, so they were there, so they could do anything, the owners could do anything with them.

> CUR-OH-03: the *shon*'s family was having visitors, and the slave that was a forefather of my mother, she was helping one of the children from the visitors. And apparently she wasn't doing it well or working fast enough and [...] the child moved the arm as if to strike the slave. And at that moment the lady from the *shon* she said, she said, no, no, no, we do not hit our slaves here.

Although this last story puts the *shon*'s wife in a good light, the fact that this instance was remarkable probably indicates that physical punishment for domestic enslaved people was common on other plantations. It is especially striking that a child felt justified in hitting the enslaved woman helping him to dress. This demonstrates an extraordinary level of entitlement and thoughtless punishment that creates at atmosphere of uncertainty for the enslaved person, which can have damaging psychological effects (Bar-Anan, Wilson, and Gilbert 2009, 123-127). However, in some situations enslaved women were able to use the circumstances of sexual abuse to increase their status in the community or to obtain resources (van der Ven 2011, 19-20).

Although the development of her teeth indicates that the Kamer van Koophandel individual was 18 years or older when she died, the rest of her body tells a different story. Stressors such as disease, hard labour, and malnutrition can cause delayed puberty and she does exhibit evidence for this: the stage of skeletal development she had reached at the time of death is more comparable to that of a 12 to 15-year-old girl. She was therefore at least three years late in terms of her pubertal development (Fricke et al. 2019). Physical immaturity may have prevented her from bearing children, but would not have protected her from the sexual abuse often perpetrated against enslaved women and may therefore have had a profound effect upon her social interactions and psychological wellbeing (Madrigal 2006, 19; Burnard 2004; Patterson 1982, 6). We should remember that she was colonised once as an African and once as a woman: this is known as *double colonisation* (Oyewumi 2006 [1997], 256-259).

Additionally, changes to the bone at the sites of several muscle attachments (principally those involved in flexion and rotation of the forearm) indicate that she was using these muscles intensively. Combined with changes to the uppermost joint of the neck and evidence for strong neck muscles, it seems that she may have been doing hard physical labour in a particularly West African (and now Curaçaoan) way: she was carrying heavy items on her head (Fricke et al. 2019).

Tiny holes on the outside of her cranium indicate that she may have suffered from a metabolic disease or dietary deficiency such as scurvy or anaemia. These lesions have a rounded aspect, which means that she was recovering from this illness, or had recovered from it when she died. Interestingly, these are the types of disease that enslaved people would have encountered on the transatlantic crossing because of the lack of adequate food (particularly fruit and vegetables). Lastly, there are several areas of her body where it is clear that new bone was being formed at the time of her death. These changes usually indicate that the individual was suffering from an active infection (Fricke et al. 2019). The overcrowded conditions of poverty and malnutrition experienced by many enslaved people would have depleted their immune systems and contributed to the spread of disease (Blakey, Rankin-Hill, Howson et al. 2009, 255-267).

After exposure to these various physical and psychological stressors, this young woman eventually died in her late teens. Unfortunately, osteoarchaeology seldom offers us the opportunity to identify exact causes of death (things that kill you usually effect soft tissues only, and archaeologists do not often have access to those), but it is unsurprising that such a stressed individual died at a young age. She was buried in unconsecrated ground, which was common for enslaved people during this period

Curaçao: A Broken Heart

(Fricke et al. 2019). An 1821 edict from the governor of Curaçao forbidding burials from taking place outside of official burial grounds seems not to have been strictly enforced (Langenfeld 2007, 129-130). This may reflect the fact that enslaved people did not have the resources to bury members of their community in official burial grounds, or alternatively that they preferred to bury their loved ones in close proximity to their living quarters, which is an Afro-Caribbean tradition (see for example Armstrong and Fleischman 2003, 33-65). Buried in the back yard of a suburban home, this young woman was probably laid to rest by other enslaved people of the same household. They may have participated in the Curaçaoan tradition of *ocho dia*, where the community gather to pray during the eight days following a burial. On the last evening, there is a party with food, drink, and storytelling. Rituals like these were an important part of group bonding which increased the ability of enslaved people to survive and resist (Lampe 2001, 126-153 140). The following section will focus on the domestic environment in which these events took place: how it was organised, and the functions it performed.

THE KUNUKU HOUSE

Figure 2.4: Traditional kunuku house at the Kas di Pal'i Maishi museum.

Source: Felicia J. Fricke.

The *kunuku* house (field or countryside house) in this picture is the one at the Kas di Pal'i Maishi living history museum. It has two rooms, a main room and a smaller bedroom to the right of the front door. Traditionally these structures are made with wattle and daub and a thatch roof, but they also include construction materials such as Dutch bricks (which arrived in Curaçao as ballast), and palm leaves. *Kas di Pal'i Maishi* actually means House of the Sorghum Stalks, and sorghum (or *maishi chikitu* in Papiamentu) was and is a staple food on the island. The front and back doors of the house align with each other, creating a through draught. This 'shotgun house' arrangement probably represents a syncretic cultural interaction between West African (Yoruba), Indigenous Caribbean, and European housing traditions (Vlach 1976b, 57-70). It indicates how enslaved people adapted their own notions of construction to a new cultural and environmental context. Yoruba houses were also arranged around an open space where most of the business of daily life was carried out, facilitating the development of close-knit families and communities (Vlach 1976a, 48-53). The household area including both indoor and outdoor spaces can be called the *homespace*, emphasising the importance of the outdoor area for community activities (Battle-Baptiste 2011: 94-101). When a kunuku house became too old to continue living in, a new house was built in front of it and the old one was used for storage (CUR-OH-03; CUR-OH-05).

It is important to visualise the homespace as the arena for many of the other activities described in this chapter. The homespace was a place where enslaved people sought to find an equilibrium between positive and negative forces. Walking around the Kas di Pal'i Maishi, one can see aloe vera plants in rows along the kunuku house walls. These plants promote positive energy. On a pole close to the house there is a pig's skull, which is intended to dispel negative energy. In the chicken coop, the feathers of the frizzled hen (which are curly and lend the hens a slightly windswept aspect) also dispel bad energy, and these hens are said to be able to detect poison (Jeanne Henriquez, personal communication). The trampled earth of the yard is very clean: sweeping this area with a broom was not only hygienic, but also kept the homespace free of negative spirits (Battle-Baptiste 2007, 233-248). Inside the house, a bowl contains indigo dye for use on the scalp (Jeanne Henriquez, personal communication), its blue colour symbolising protection. The aloe vera, the pig skull, the frizzled hens, the blue dye, and the swept yard are part of a network of protective elements which hold the enslaved homespace together. The construction and maintenance of this network could allow enslaved people to feel that they had some control over their circumstances, which is very psychologically important for feelings of hope and willingness to survive (Lima, de Souza, and Sene 2014, 103-136).

The supernatural network of the homespace is related to Curaçaoan beliefs about medicine. It is not enough to treat only physical symptoms: spiritual problems relating to the balance of good and evil must also be addressed, in a type of holistic medicine (see CUR-OH-07 and Allen 2010, 221-228). In order to treat physical symptoms, enslaved people could use plants such as aloe vera, oregano, rosemary, passionflower (*corona de la birgen* in Papiamentu) and string bush (*Cordia cylindrostachya*, known as *basora pretu* in Papiamentu):

> CUR-OH-06: *Corona de la birgen* that's a very good plant, you can boil it, you can use it on your skin.

> CUR-OH-04.2: But the *basora pretu* was very good if you have, let's say, diarrhoea. And it will help you. So my grandfather for instance, the moment that he saw a bush of *basora pretu* he used to take of his hat, tip his hat, because he had a kind of respect for the plant

The homespace was therefore a site of recovery, belief, and agency which enslaved people actively created in order to survive. The following section will dive further into the beliefs of enslaved people and how these related to hardship and survival.

LA VIRGEN DEL VALLE

The following photograph shows a mid-20th century glass candle holder, found in the ruins of a late-19th century kunuku house in the enslaved village at Plantation Knip (also known as Kenepa) (Haviser 1999, 221-263). It bears a picture of a woman in elaborate clothing and the words *La Virgen del Valle* (The Virgin of the Valley). This incarnation of the Virgin Mary is very popular in Venezuela and is associated with bringing rain (Infomistico 2018). It is understandable that residents of arid Curaçao might feel affinity with this particular Virgin Mary. They have certainly had several hundred years of close contact with Venezuela in which to learn about her. From the early 18th century onwards, the Venezuelan town of Coro was a popular destination for enslaved people escaping Curaçao not only because it was nearby but also because the Spanish Crown might grant them their freedom as fellow Catholics. The growing Curaçaoan population in Coro helped to facilitate a vibrant smuggling network (especially in cacao, tobacco, and hides) between the island and the mainland (Rupert 2012: 167, 197-198).

These international links allowed enslaved people in Curaçao to learn about resistance in other parts of the Caribbean. The Tula Revolt of 1795, which was the largest uprising of enslaved people in the history of the island, occurred just three months after a rebellion also took place in Coro (Fatah-Black 2013, 35-60). Indeed, significant contacts between the island and the mainland continue to this day. Until recently, the island relied on fruit imports which came in by boat to the floating market in Willemstad, as well as on Venezuelan oil which went to the Willemstad refinery. Now, the social and political unrest in Venezuela is causing trade difficulties, but it has also encouraged Venezuelans to enter Curaçao as immigrants, a reversal of the historical migration which saw enslaved people seek safety on the mainland (Broere 2019; Redactie 2019).

Figure 2.5: Candle holder from the Kenepa/Knip village showing the Virgin Mary (La Virgen del Valle).

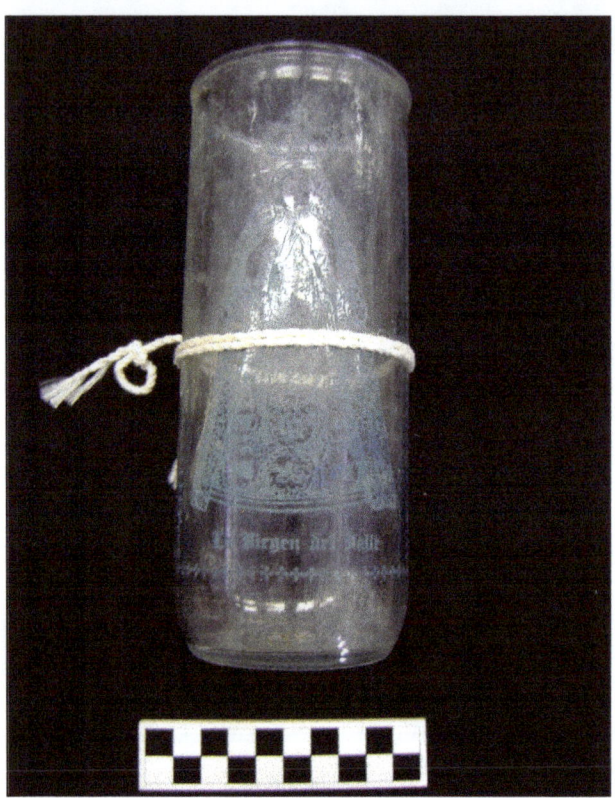

Source: Felicia J. Fricke.

Catholicism was one of the most important Venezuelan influences on Curaçao. Priests from Venezuela were permitted to come and convert the enslaved population of the island. It was very successful: when slavery was abolished by the Dutch in 1863, 86% of the island population was Catholic (Oostindie 2005: 40). Enslaved people may have been attracted to Catholicism because of its therapeutic effects, and the European elites of Curaçao, who were often Dutch Protestants or Portuguese Jews, encouraged this because it helped to maintain the line between Black and white (Oostindie 1995, 143-178). In their view, this line was constantly being threatened because of the comparatively large numbers of free Afro-Curaçaoans making up the island's population. This situation had arisen from the frequent manumission of enslaved people, practised by slave owners for economic reasons. In times of drought or economic decline, it was much cheaper to manumit enslaved people than to look after them (Oostindie 2011, 1-22). This resulted in old, disabled, or unwell people being abandoned in the *mondi* (bush) to fend for themselves (CUR-OH-07). Manumission did not therefore always represent an increase in quality of life. Freed individuals might continue to experience high levels of uncertainty associated with the threat of re-enslavement (see Hoonhout and Mareite 2018).

There was also a second reason that the European elites of Curaçao were in favour of conversion to Catholicism: as mentioned above, it could be used as a tool for making enslaved people (and later free Afro-Curaçaoan people) obedient and loyal by encouraging them to accept their social position (Oostindie 2005: 19, 40-41). Indeed, in modern times psychologists have noted that religious beliefs can reinforce maladaptive behaviour in certain circumstances, for example fasting becoming intertwined with eating disorders (Spangler 2010, 358-370).

> CUR-OH-06: It gives you hope and I mean […] let's say you're being beaten every day and then somebody tells you […] at the end of it you go to paradise. You know and that gives people strength.

> CUR-OH-02: the Catholic Church has made us very docile. You know? Very passive. And that in that aspect the Catholic Church has collaborated with the colonial power.

In 1824, a Dutch priest called Martinus Niewindt introduced a new structure of community living based around schools and other Catholic organisations, which was designed to control the enslaved population by restricting social movement and encouraging obedience (Lampe 2001, 126-153: 131, 144-145). As a racist and sexist institution, slavery was able to benefit from this involvement of the Catholic Church, which had a particularly oppressive impact upon Afro-Curaçaoan women who were socially excluded if they did not conform. They were encouraged to live the *bida drechi* (respectable life), for example by being monogamous and conforming to the European ideal of the nuclear family (Allen 2017a, 99-112). This type of social organisation was not necessarily comfortable for enslaved people, who may have come from societies where men and women live apart (CUR-OH-03). African-descendant women have been similarly targeted elsewhere in the Americas, for example being presented as bad mothers if they tried to obtain economic security through relationships with white men (Ono-George 2017, 356-372). Inherent in this focus on Catholicism and an idealised European concept of respectability was the destruction of Curaçaoan traditional culture:

> CUR-OH-07: [The Catholic Church] also tried to change their mind, to change their religion, to break their drums, instead of helping them, standing by them, to do their culture.

Slave owners, for example, discouraged enslaved people from dancing the African-style *tambú,* which included erotic moves and political commentary which were threatening to European social mores and the stability of societal structure (CUR-OH-02; CUR-OH-03; CUR-OH-07; CUR-OH-08) (see Rosalia 1997). Interestingly, while supressing other Afro-Curaçaoan cultural elements, the Catholic Church communicated with enslaved people in Papiamentu. This was the language that most enslaved people felt comfortable in and was therefore a good medium for spiritual education, but denying enslaved people the opportunity to learn Dutch was also part of a system of gatekeeping that separated the African and European descendant populations (Roe 2016: 77, 90). Equally, the rejection of the Papiamentu language by the governmental authorities had a profound negative impact upon the Afro-Curaçaoan population into the 20th century (Fouse 2002: 137-158).

Despite this hostile cultural atmosphere, Afro-Curaçaoan communities were able to combine African traditions with Catholic ones to generate a unique creole religious culture (Allen 2007: 237-250). This is still observable in modern celebrations such as *Lele Toni* (the day of St Anthony), which is celebrated with dancing and during which the statue of St Anthony and his (non-canonical) child is decorated with candles, fruits, bread, and rum. During this celebration people ask St Anthony for money, marriage, and eternal salvation (CUR-OH-08) (Brenneker 2017a: 15-16). This celebration contains strong elements of both Catholicism and *brua* or *montamentu,* which are complementary parts of an African-influenced Curaçaoan belief system (van der Ven 2011: 87). *Brua* is associated with witchcraft and stimulates rather negative reactions because of its intent to harm (CUR-OH-06; CUR-OH-07; CUR-OH-08) while *montamentu* is seen as more benevolent and linked to the ancestors.

> CUR-OH-07:   ...*montamentu* is a ceremony in which people come together and they seek contact with their ancestors. And they come together and they drink and they eat and they dance and [...] then some of them would get really completely possessed by that ancestor, they began to speak different languages and begin to dance like snakes, and also that through *montamentu* you can help people who are sick.

Religious objects designed to assist with the maintenance of the positive and negative power balance between ancestors and spirits include portable amulets. One of the artefacts from Kenepa village is a shiny, reflective glass perfume bottle stopper. Shiny or glittery surfaces resemble water which in some West African cultures (and in the Americas) is seen as a liminal medium where life and death meet (Kamash 2008, 224-237). Such objects may therefore be used to attract positive spirits (Lima, de Souza, and Sene 2014, 103-136). Alternatively, they can be intended as *apotropaics* (objects that repel evil) (Wilkie 1997, 81-106). Copper objects are also occasionally recorded as potential amulets (Lima, de Souza, and Sene 2014, 103-136). A copper bell from Kenepa village may also therefore have been used as an amulet with an additional auditory dimension.

White conch shells (*Strombus gigas*) can also represent the world of the ancestors within and beyond the sea, an Angolan concept (Farris Thompson 1990, 148-184). However, they can also be used for other more mundane purposes, such as wind instruments and doorstops (Haviser 1999, 221-263). Today they are a protected species, and because they are a local delicacy they are still in danger from poachers (Dutch Caribbean Nature Alliance 2014). The following section will explore the gustatory traditions of Curaçao in more detail.

DATU AND KADUSHI

Figure 2.6: View of the plantation house at Knip.

Source: Felicia J. Fricke.

This photograph shows Plantation Knip at the western end of Curaçao in May 2016. The big house (seen to the right of the photograph) is now a museum. Out of frame to the right are a small cluster of storehouses, and on the other side of the wall to the left are some pens which used to hold goats. Beyond the goat pens is the village, which has been continually inhabited for hundreds of years: first by enslaved people, then by people living under the *paga tera* labour system until 1974, and now by their free descendants (Kas di Kultura 2008; Haviser 1995). The plantation house, which is on a hill, easily overlooks the village and thereby allowed the plantation owners to assert control over the enslaved people by making them feel that they were constantly observed. This device is called the *Panopticon* and has also been used in institutions such as schools and prisons all over the world (Miller and Miller 1987, 3-29).

Plantations in Curaçao grew subsistence crops and reared animals, and owners treated their plantations somewhat like country estates (Rupert 2012: 135). Agriculture on the island was made especially difficult by the climatic and geological conditions (CUR-OH-07). One interviewee also referred to the sharp nature of the rocks and plants in Curaçao:

> CUR-OH-06: The soil is very hard, our soil is very hard to dig in [...and] we've got a lot of spikes. If you don't have shoes - that must have been very painful! And even the rocks, a lot of the rocks of course are very pointy. How does one walk on these things?

Indeed, enslaved people in Curaçao were allowed to wear shoes, unlike those in Suriname (van der Dijs 2011: 127). According to this oral historical account, however, it was probably not precisely a kindness but rather a necessity to avoid enslaved people becoming injured and unproductive. This is a good example of the way a postcolonial theoretical approach and the use of oral history can turn established narratives on their head.

Plantation Knip was probably established in the late 17th century, but the large *landhuis* (plantation house) and outbuildings were constructed in the 18th century, with additions and alterations in the early 19th century (Kas di Kultura 2008; de Palm 1985: 291-293). It became one of the largest and most productive estates on the island, engaged in a diverse range of activities including animal husbandry (cows, sheep, goats, turkeys, chickens, geese, and pigeons) for meat and wool; the growth of Brazil wood and indigo for export; and the cultivation of provisions such as sorghum, beans, pumpkins, watermelons, mangoes, and lemons. Some of the fruit trees can still be seen growing close to the *landhuis* (Kas di Kultura 2008). This site looms large in the national consciousness of Curaçao because it was the starting location of the abovementioned 1795 Tula Revolt, when thousands of enslaved people and free Afro-Curaçaoans in the western part of the island refused to work, marched towards Willemstad, fought against colonial forces, and were eventually defeated or executed (do Rego 2009, 27-35). This important historical event is echoed in the events of *trinta di mei* (30th May) 1969, when thousands of mine and refinery workers protested again unfair labour conditions and set fire to buildings in Willemstad (Anderson and Dynes 1975: 4). Both of these events have been credited with having an important impact on improvements in working conditions on the island.

To the extreme left of the Knip photograph is a tall, branching cactus. This type of cactus (*Cereus repandus*) is called *kadushi* in Papiamentu and is used to make soup (CUR-OH-04). The kadushi looks very similar to another cactus (*Stenocereus griseus*) which is called *datu* in Papiamentu and is used to make double-layer fences which are very effective against goats. The kadushi has a trunk and therefore looks more like a tree, while the datu has slightly curving branches which rise straight from the ground.

The consumption of kadushi is part of a Curaçaoan culinary tradition which developed during the era of slavery through the incorporation of traditions from many different cultures, including Indigenous, African, Jewish, and European influences. Iguana, fish, pumpkin, papaya, and cactus were all food sources native to the Americas while sorghum and okra were originally African. A typically Curaçaoan meal is *funchi* (a type of polenta made with sorghum) and *kabritu* (goat, made into a stew) but there was also an emphasis on one-pot meals, cooked on three stones over a fire and then shared out into individual portions (CUR-OH-02; CUR-OH-03). The one-pot nature and sharing culture of Curaçaoan foodways is also an aspect of its altruistic tradition, which contributed to community survival (see CUR-OH-02). A communal approach to foodways is often observed amongst groups with limited resource access (see for example Wallman 2014, 45-68).

Many of the most important foodstuffs were available in the mondi or along the coastline (for example cacti, whelks, and crabs) and were therefore cheap and easy to obtain (see CUR-OH-08). The exploitation of multiple resources (hunted, foraged, gathered, grown, fished, and stolen) made enslaved people more able to cope with changing and uncertain circumstances, such as periodic drought. It is worth noting here that the historian AF Paula (1987: 19) refers to the gardens where enslaved people grew their food as 'satisfying'. I would like you to consider an alternative viewpoint: that these gardens, while indeed providing a certain degree of independence, may also have introduced an extra source of stress, since they represented yet another area of work to be done on top of that dictated by the overseers. In the next section, we follow an enslaved man to his burial site near the Willemstad wharf, and explore the types of work that he and other enslaved people did.

FLEUR DE MARIE

The map below shows Willemstad in 1906. The neighbourhood of Scharloo can be seen to the north of the Waaigat. From the end of the 17th century, the western part of Scharloo near Sint Annabaai was occupied by merchants and sailors who benefitted from a position close to the waterfront. Housing development further to the east along the northern bank of the Waaigat began in the 1850s, when rich Jewish families started to build houses there (Victorina and Kraan 2012). The western part of Scharloo close to the wharf area includes a neighbourhood called Fleur de Marie. In 2011, the skeleton of a male individual was recovered there – two individuals had already been uncovered in the same area in 1993 (Victorina and Kraan 2012; Haviser 1993). Carbon dating (AMS) combined with the archaeological context indicate that the 2011 individual probably died between 1780 and 1800 (Victorina and Kraan

2012). His remains are important for our understanding of the lifeways of enslaved people in Curaçao because they help to demonstrate the wide range of activities in which enslaved people were involved, and the social context in which these activities happened.

The current neighbourhood of Fleur de Marie is situated on land that used to belong to Scharloo Plantation, established by the WIC in 1634. In 1729 this plantation was divided into pieces and sold off for housing because it was too dry for profitable agriculture (Victorina and Kraan 2012). After the death of a landowner called Willem Jansz Vermeulen in 1753, his daughter Neeltje inherited a strip of Scharloo land reaching from the wharves to the hill Berg Altena at the other end of the main road. On this land were a house called Bellevue or Klijn Versailles and at least two tombs. The stretch of land probably included Fleur de Marie as it encompassed nearly all the land to the north of the road (Winkel 1987: 6). This indicates that before the death and burial of the 2011 individual, people had already been buried on this empty land.

Figure 2.7: Early 20th century map of Willemstad showing the neighbourhood of Scharloo.

Source: Werbata 1906. Courtesy of Harrie Verstappen (vrcurassow.com).

As an individual of African ancestry living in Curaçao during the 18th century, he was likely at the bottom of the social hierarchy (Goslinga 1979: 112). Indeed, he was several centimetres shorter than enslaved men in comparative populations from the US, although of a similar height to enslaved men in the Caribbean during the early 19th century (see Carson 2008, 812-831; Margo and Steckel 1982, 516-538; Higman 1979, 373-386). Low stature is often associated with low social status because poverty, disease and malnourishment can all prevent people from attaining their full potential height (DeWitte and Hughes-Morey 2012, 1412-1419).

Burial on marginal, unconsecrated land so close to the developing suburb of Scharloo and the shipping activities beside St Annabaai suggests that he was involved in the life of one of these areas. For example, he could have been a domestic servant in one of the houses on the southern side of Scharlooweg, or perhaps even at Bellevue itself. Alternatively, he may have been a sailor working on the nearby wharves: enslaved people in Curaçao were sometimes granted temporary manumission to go to sea and earn money for their masters (Rupert 2012: 103-104).

Sailors during this time period were at risk of getting scurvy (vitamin C deficiency). In the mid-18th century a Scottish doctor called James Lind discovered that citrus fruits could cure scurvy, but it was half a century later that organisations such as the British Navy regularly took these on board to prevent and/or counteract it (Baron 2009, 315-332). Sailors during the second half of the 18th century were therefore still vulnerable to the disease. Symptoms include bleeding gums and eventual tooth loss, and there are also other changes to the skeleton caused by bleeding under the periosteum (the membrane which surrounds the bones), which can be observed when someone has had scurvy for a long period of time, especially increased bone porosity and the formation of new bone (Snoddy et al. 2018, 1-20). The individual from Fleur de Marie had lost all but one of his teeth at the time of death and healing porous lesions (porotic hyperostosis) were visible on the bones of his skull. *Porotic hyperostosis* is porosity of the external aspect of the cranial bones caused by increased red blood cell production when there is blood loss or the red blood cells are not functioning properly, for example in cases of anaemia, scurvy, or malaria (Snoddy et al. 2018, 1-20; Smith-Guzman 2015, 624-635; Walker et al. 2009, 109-125). In the environment of slavery it is not unexpected that enslaved individuals display porotic hyperostosis. There is plenty of evidence that their diet was often inadequate (Kiple and Kiple 1991 [1980], 173-182).

Indeed, tooth loss can be related to the consumption of sugary or high carbohydrate diets which encourage the development of cavities. The last remaining tooth of the Fleur de Marie individual does have one cavity at the gum line and is extremely worn on the biting surface. This type of wear occurs over time due to the consumption of gritty food, and is therefore more extreme in older individuals (see Teaford and Lytle 1996, 143-147; Brothwell 1981: 71-72). In Curaçao, the staple carbohydrate *maishi chikitu* (sorghum) is traditionally prepared using a stone *mano* (pestle) and *metate* (mortar) (Jeanne Henriquez, personal communication). This introduces grit into the food, which wears down the teeth. It is therefore likely that this diet caused the cavity and wear that can be seen on his last remaining tooth. It is also possible to obtain other information about his diet. Isotopic analysis of teeth can determine what kinds of food an individual consumed while their teeth were forming (because of how certain isotopes are present in higher levels at the top of the food chain), and the 2011 individual consumed a diet roughly equal in marine and terrestrial foods (Victorina and Kraan 2012). This fits well with what we know about the diets of enslaved people from historical and archaeological sources.

Much of the work of fishermen and shipbuilders also took place in the Willemstad harbour area (Rupert 2012: 3). Those who sold surplus or handicrafts (such as fish and straw hats) in the market or were hired out for a fee might be allowed to keep some of the money from such activities, and work towards earning their freedom (Allen 2007: 73, 203; Schiltkamp, Smit, and Wachlin 2000: 21). Historians have noted that craftsmen and enslaved people engaged in independent labour also had more freedom of movement than those who were enslaved on the plantations (Roitman 2017, 399-417; Jordaan 2013: 52-53). Enslaved people residing in Willemstad might even be permitted to live apart from their owner, and this afforded them a greater degree of autonomy (Rupert 2012: 3, 125, 129). Interviewees in this study (CUR-OH-02; CUR-OH-06; CUR-OH-07) confirmed that those with certain occupations such as carpenters, sailors, vendors, and messengers could earn some money, engage in the economy, and be more independently mobile (see for example Langenfeld 2010: 63; Schiltkamp, Smit, and Wachlin 2000: 21). However, they stressed that this did not necessarily improve the conditions of slavery as a whole:

> CUR-OH-06: [the artisans] had a slight[ly] different experience because they could earn their own money, but of course they had to give some of the money to their owners. But it's, again, I'm not saying it was better. I'm just saying it was different.

> CUR-OH-02: there were fathers and grandfathers who would buy the freedom of a son or a nephew or whatever, a family member. And that is very interesting, to see how men have, you know, through the process of enslavement they have not succumbed, you know, have been very resilient.

Investigating evidence for different types of occupation or labour on the human skeleton is notoriously difficult, and skeletal changes that can be caused by activity can also often be caused by normal skeletal degeneration as a person ages (Jurmain et al. 2012, 531-552). In this case, rough areas of bone at muscle attachment sites on the humerus (upper arm) and tibia (lower leg) of the 2011 individual may indicate trauma or repeated microtrauma in these areas. These muscles are involved in flexing, extending, rotating, and abducting the arm, and flexion of the feet (Stone and Stone 2009: 123, 197). The arms in particular are involved in 'voluntary' movements associated with occupation (Villotte and Knusel 2014, 168-174; Ponce 2012, 71-85).

However, changes to several of this individual's joints, especially the hips, may indeed be associated with age rather than occupation. The hips are one of the most common sites for arthritis because they are weight-bearing (Roberts and Manchester 2010: 138; Waldron 1997, 186-189).

The 2011 individual from Fleur de Marie survived to an age where he would have been dependent on those around him for his survival. Discomfort from his hips would have made it difficult for him to participate in certain types of strenuous physical activity, while his mostly edentulous mouth required the provision of soft food. Although he may have endured extreme hardship, his survival into old age demonstrates resilience in a community battling social, economic, and environmental adversity. Resourcefulness in this environment will now be discussed below.

STAINLESS STEEL

This photograph shows a mid-20th century stainless steel knife from the kunuku house at Kenepa village. Knives like this usually have a much longer blade: this one has clearly been used so often that the blade has been shortened almost by half. The use of such objects beyond the span of their normal life is common in contexts of resource scarcity. People surviving in such conditions often use a variety of mechanisms to acquire all the objects and resources that they need for everyday life. These mechanisms could include theft, home manufacture, and engagement with the economy.

Figure 2.8: Worn stainless steel knife from the Kenepa/Knip village.

Source: Felicia J. Fricke.

Domestic items (such as bowls and spoons) were often made from perishable materials, especially calabash (*Crescentia cujete*), an important traditional resource (Veeris 2017). Artefacts at the Kas di Pal'i Maishi include a food mixer made from a twig, clothes made from old rice and flour bags, and a trumpet made from a cow horn. These objects demonstrate a high level of self-sufficiency. Another example of such resourcefulness is the use of household or agricultural items such as ploughshares as musical instruments (Haviser 1999, 221-263).

There was also evidence for the occasional luxury item. Glass drinking vessels and fine porcelain found at Kenepa indicate interaction in the economy. However, the stainless-steel knife does indicate that inhabitants were not always able to replace old household items. Reuse is often thought to indicate resource scarcity and economic change in artefact biography contexts (see Swift 2012, 167-215; Wilson 1995, 126-140). All the diverse ways in which enslaved people obtained or maintained goods can be seen as acts of resistance because they involve not only defiance and resourcefulness but also the development of social and economic networks.

It was also necessary for enslaved people to develop coping mechanisms which were psychological rather than physical. These included escapist practices such as storytelling, music and dance, and alcohol consumption. Alcohol can be a very effective coping mechanism in the short term, although it can also be maladaptive because of its potentially negative side effects (see for example Prost, Lemieux, and Ai 2016, 825-844; Merrill and Thomas 2013, 1672-1678). At Kenepa village and the Kas di Pal'i Maishi there were a variety of alcohol-related items including shot glasses and stoneware gin bottles. However, it is also possible that these bottles were used for other purposes such as carrying water or for storage (see Espersen 2019; Odewale and Hardy 2019).

Storytelling was another important escapist coping strategy, which also provided education and comfort. The most well-known stories told in Curaçao are those about the spider Kompa Nanzi (known elsewhere as Anansi), West African stories that have enormous cultural importance within and beyond Curaçao. Hausa (from Niger and Nigeria) and Fante Twi people (Ghana and Ivory Coast) tell similar stories (Dalphinis 1985: 165), as do people in the SSS islands (St Eustatius, St Maarten and Saba) (Albus 2001, 443-447; Sypkens-Smit 1981: 46) and St Lucia (Dalphinis 1985: 165). These stories are often concerned with the triumph of a small animal over larger animals through the use of clever tricks, which must have resonated with enslaved people wishing to triumph over their owners. The stories also had moral functions relating directly to the circumstances of slavery, for example:

> CUR-OH-05: Cha Tiger and Kompa Nanzi they asked Cha Candela - Cha Candela is the Cha Fire - Cha Fire, dance for me, I want to see you dance! And Cha Candela, Fire, said, no I will not dance because my dance is very, very ugly. No, just once, just once! Dance, dance! Look at we all dancing. Cha Fire said no I will not dance because my dance is very, very dangerous, it's very, very ugly. So they force him to dance then they start to dance and then he burn down the whole community. [laughs] So. Don't force people, if they say no, OK, fine. So. That came not from my mother, it was grandmother.

> CUR-OH-05: [Nanzi] is always winning. He would fool his wife and kids! [laughs] He is too smart. [It shows] how just a common person can fool a king.

Another important story describes a return to Africa. In this story, there is a certain group of people called the Guene (also the name of the second creole language of Curaçao, now no longer spoken, but which had much stronger African influences than Papiamentu) who have wings and can fly back to Africa as long as they have not eaten salt (CUR-OH-03). This story is symbolic of escape, either physically or perhaps spiritually in the form of suicide (Allen 2017b, 281-295). However, it has a particularly tragic undertone because it includes those who were not able to fly back. It therefore has both hopeful and heartbreakingly sad connotations.

> I heard that the Guenes had wings, but this lady did not have any. All those who had wings flew away. She stayed and worked in Santa Barbara. She stayed back because she had eaten salt. That is why she stayed back. *(Allen 2007: 69)*

Music and dance could also act as a form of release. The role of tambú in social and political commentary is similar to that of calypso in other areas of the Caribbean such as Trinidad (see Finden-Crofts 1998, 147-166). Songs provided encouragement and helped to counteract or temporarily escape internalised negative self-image (Allen 2001, 421-429) and were used to give strength during work (CUR-OH-09) and to relay important information (CUR-OH-04; CUR-OH-07). They mentioned topics such as escape, migration, leisure and work activities, and scandal, and could also be lullabies (Brenneker 2017b: 17-20; Allen 2001, 421-429). They undermined psychological attempts to dominate and divide enslaved people and helped to organise rebellions such as the 1795 Tula Revolt (CUR-OH-04.2).

> CUR-OH-07: singing give you also power to forget the bad moments of the day. While you sing you can express your feelings [...] Tambú I think the second thing that was important in their lives to survive.

> CUR-OH-04: we call it the tambú. [...] you would always, you know, bring an anecdote or something that your master did. But they put it in a kind of a song and everyone thought, oh, that's nice, it sounds nice, but it was a way of, you know, expressing violence, aggressiveness.

Laughing at the slave owners behind their backs, as occurred during the tambú, was a method of resistance (Paula 1987: 31). Psychological coping mechanisms used by Curaçaoan descendants of enslaved people also included dissemblance (avoiding talking about painful subjects) and humour (Allen 2017a, 99-112). Indeed, interviewees mentioned dissemblance by older generations who were temporally closer to slavery (CUR-OH-07).

In many contexts around the world, but especially in the context of slavery, literacy can also be a powerful act of resistance (JanMohamed 2010, 139-155). Artefacts relating to literacy have been found in enslaved contexts in the Americas, for example at Maria Franklin's (2017: 121) excavation of the mid-18th century enslaved quarters at Coke's Plantation, Virginia, as well as at the Kenepa village kunuku house in Curaçao. The Catholic Church was instrumental in the education of the Afro-Curaçaoan population after 1863. The education they offered had an intentionally limited effect, but it did allow some people to get jobs and earn money (Abraham-van der Mark 2001, 625-631).

Enslaved people could also escape Curaçao, and by various means unavailable to those on other islands. An example of this is the temporary manumission bestowed by owners in order to allow their enslaved people to go to sea (Rupert 2012: 103-104). It was intended that the temporarily manumitted individuals would return to Curaçao and become enslaved once more at the end of their voyage, but in reality many used this as an opportunity to escape. Those who returned were likely to do so because they did not want to leave their family behind (Allen 2012, 51-65). The contraband networks connecting Curaçao to Venezuela also provided opportunities for escape (Rupert 2012: 197). Enslaved people took the opportunity to run away even when the prospect of freedom was just around the corner.

> CUR-OH-05: a brother of my grand-grand-mother also, let's say he run away and he run away, I think, just two years before abolition of the slavery.

There is also plenty of documentary evidence for this because advertisements for the recapture of runaway enslaved people were posted in local newspaper *De Curaçaosche Courant* (Langenfeld 2010: 68). Their desire to run away even when abolition was so close indicates that to the enslaved people of Curaçao, the absence of a sugar economy like that of Suriname was not sufficient reason to stay. As AF Paula (1968: 24) has observed, enslaved people did not experience their circumstances in relative context. The following section will address the plantation context during the post-abolition period, when Afro-Curaçaoans still experienced the social conditions of enslavement, some of which still have a tangible legacy today.

VEERIS PLANTATION

In the photograph below you can see the face of an Indigenous Caribbean ancestry man, one of two men buried in the late 19th or early 20th century. The area where they were buried now lies under the large Sambil shopping centre to the northwest of Willemstad, but it used to be part of Veeris or Union Plantation, an 1820s amalgamation of the plantations *Drie Gebroeders*, *Westerveld*, and *Eendracht*. 'Veeris' was the family name of the first known owners of Drie Gebroeders and

Westerveld plantations (Curacao Monuments 2006). The burials are just a five-minute walk from the landhuis, which was built in the early 19th century (Huijers and Ezechiels 1992: 148). Enslaved cemeteries and enslaved villages were often close to each other, and if the village was located near these burials then the plantation layout would conform to Bentham's *Panopticon*, with the enslaved community under the eye of the plantation owner (see Miller and Miller 1987, 3-29). These individuals are important for our understanding of the lifeways of enslaved people because they date from the period immediately before or immediately after the abolition of slavery, when the social state of slavery often persisted. The various pathologies that they have are useful in demonstrating the kinds of work-related dangers present in the Curaçaoan work environment (Fricke & Laffoon, 2019).

Figure 2.9: The skull of a man buried at Veeris Plantation in the late 19th or early 20th century.

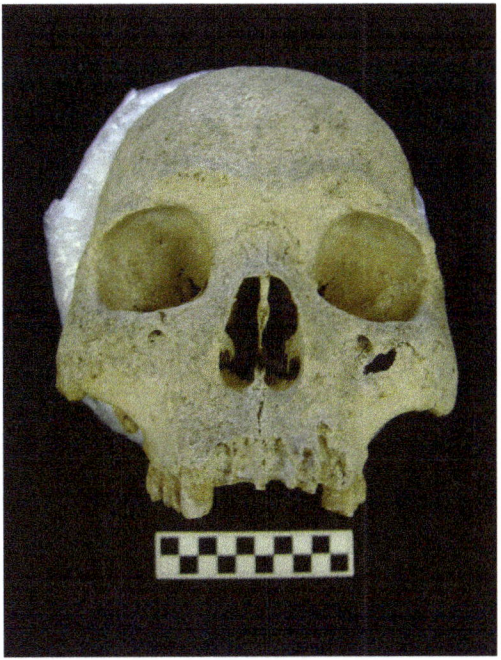

Source: Felicia J. Fricke.

By the early 19th century, Curaçao was no longer a thriving commercial hub. The United States had emerged as the new centre for American trade, and many of the Spanish colonies in South America, including Venezuela, had gained independence. For the next century the island remained an economic backwater (Rupert 2012: 245-246). In 1863 the approximately 7000 people still living in slavery in Curaçao were legally freed, but social and economic conditions continued to be harsh for the freed population (Allen 2014, 39-56). The paga tera labour system introduced in 1863 tied people to the plantations and forced them to work for free, and many were left in poverty (Allen 2007: 121, 133-141). Afro-Curaçaoans still existed in a space where both social and literal death were part of the landscape. At this point it is useful to think about a theory put forward by the literature expert and postcolonialist Abdul JanMohamed. In his book *The Death-Bound-Subject*, he explores how African-Americans living both before and after the date of abolition experienced (and in some cases still experience) a society which oppressed them using the threat of death (JanMohamed 2005: 5). This meant, using the philosopher Giorgio Agamben's concept of *bare life*, that African-American people could be killed with impunity: the lynch mob took on sovereign power (JanMohamed 2005: 8-9). The slave master (or lynch mob) was able to appropriate death as a mode of control, as enslaved people or people living in bare life exist under a commuted death sentence for which the perpetrator will not face serious consequences (JanMohamed 2005: 15). This does not necessarily imply that the victim has no socio-political agency (Hamilakis 2016, 121-139). Rather, bare life is just one possible facet of adversity that subalterns may encounter and against which they may resist. For example, we see the concept of bare life at work in the narrative of Frederick Douglass, who was enslaved in the early 19th century in Maryland. He recounts a fight with his cruel master Mr Covey:

> He asked me if I meant to persist in my resistance. I told him I did, come what might; that he had used me like a brute for six months, and that I was determined to be used so no longer. [...] The whole six months afterwards, that I spent with Mr Covey, he never laid the weight of his finger upon me in anger. [...] This battle with Mr Covey was the turning-point in my career as a slave. It rekindled the few expiring embers of freedom, and revived within me a sense of my own manhood. [...] The gratification afforded by the triumph was a full compensation for whatever else might follow, even death itself. *(Douglass 2013: 58-59)*

By embracing his potential death, Frederick Douglass was able to obtain a certain amount of power over his owner. He had identified the inherent contradiction in enslavement: it is the wish to remain alive at all costs that enslaves you, but the owner is unwilling to follow through on the threat of death because death is unproductive (JanMohamed 2010, 139-155). The relationship between enslavement and death, and between death and bare life in lynch mob victims, links the lives of enslaved and free people in a way that continues today, for example in sex trafficking, forced labour, and the murder of civilians by police. This entanglement of the past and the present is noted by theorists of contemporary archaeology, who argue that the past is always present both physically and psychologically (Moshenska and Gonzalez-Ruibal 2015, 1-17). This clearly has great relevance to the study of Caribbean slavery involving oral historical testimonies and engaging with issues of mental slavery and inherited trauma (Thomas, D. 2016, 177-200).

After abolition, paga tera was not the only way that the state was able to control Afro-Curaçaoan people. New laws against vagrancy meant that homeless and unemployed people could effectively be kidnapped and sentenced to hard labour (Allen 2007: 122-123). Across the Caribbean, there was a period of transition from slavery to emancipation (Finneran 2016, 388-405). This is still continuing today (Haviser 2001).

> CUR-OH-07: The slave - slave? Kind of slave! [laughs] - had to work for the slave owner. So it's kind of slavery but in another way. You were free really but the problem was that you're free but you had nothing and so you had to come back to the *shon* ... it was like a kind of extension of slavery really, really. And I think that it was... [...] it was planned, it was conscious, it was... in the system. Part of the system.

The Indigenous Caribbean ancestry man from Veeris worked in the paga tera system and experienced the psychological and physical effects of continued oppression. He had bilateral osteochondritis dissecans at the distal femora (knee), indicating that he may have performed hard labour in adolescence, like the young woman from the Kamer van Koophandel (Kessler et al. 2014, 320-326). Other evidence from the skeleton shows that hard labour may have continued throughout his life, as he developed widespread arthritis and degenerative joint disease (Roberts and Manchester 2010: 143). A large bony growth restricted movement between the first and second lumbar vertebrae in the lower part of his spine (possibly secondary to a fracture), and this would have had an impact on his mobility. He also had a healed misaligned fracture to the right zygomatic arch (cheekbone) (Fricke & Laffoon, 2019). Fractures to the facial region like this have been associated with episodes of abuse in both modern and archaeological populations (Gowland 2016, 514-523), and with hand-to-hand combat (Walker 1997, 145-179). In a plantation context, this injury does not necessarily indicate that he did any fighting himself. He may have been subjected to these injuries as punishment by a *fitó* (overseer), *bomba* (slave driver), or *shon* (master) (Fricke & Laffoon, 2019). Alternatively, the injury could have been inflicted during an accident, for example an encounter with a large animal, since the plantation was known primarily for raising livestock (Huijers and Ezechiels 1992: 148). However, it is also possible that he was employed as a domestic servant. Creole enslaved people like this man from Veeris Plantation were sometimes preferred for domestic tasks, perhaps because their often lighter skin was perceived as more attractive or because they were more familiar with Papiamentu (Paula 1987: 16-17).

There was an Indigenous Caquetio population present in Curaçao when the Dutch took the island from the Spanish in 1634 (Hoonhout and Mareite 2018; Rupert 2012: 3, 21, 36), and they have had a noticeable impact upon various aspects of Curaçaoan culture in a way that has not happened in all areas of the Caribbean. For example, the shelters that enslaved people used to hide from the midday sun when they worked in the fields, or that they used to keep seeds safe from rodents, were constructed using an Indigenous design (Jeanne Henriquez, personal communication). Apart from the abovementioned influences on Curaçaoan cuisine, there are also several Papiamentu words of Indigenous origin, for example *awakati* (avocado) and *hamaka* (hammock) (CUR-OH-09). This individual from Veeris therefore represents an under-discussed facet of Curaçaoan heritage and a population group suffering the same types of oppression as African-descendant individuals (Fricke & Laffoon, 2019).

Another individual buried at this site (an adult possible male) had slightly asymmetrical clavicles, which may indicate physical labour including uneven loading across the shoulders (Mays, Steele, and Ford 1999, 18-28). As a labourer on a plantation that specialised in *veeteelt* (animal husbandry), there are many tasks that could have required such asymmetrical loading. These include carrying and restraining animals. Close encounters with these animals could also have caused the misaligned healed fracture to his right tibia (Fricke & Laffoon, 2019). In modern populations, fractures of the tibia are caused by direct force or by twisting forces in individuals who often run, dance, or jump (Dandy and Edwards 2003: 256-258). This fracture was subsequently complicated by osteomyelitis, an infection of the bone marrow which causes an extreme response of bone growth and pus production. The pus is usually drained from the bone marrow through a naturally forming *cloaca*, or hole. This would have considerably affected his quality of life by causing pain and restricting movement (Djuric-Srejic and Roberts 2001, 311-320).

This individual also had new bone formation in both maxillary sinuses (Fricke & Laffoon, 2019). This is known as *sinusitis*, and is an infection that may have been caused by the inhalation of smoke and dust in the dry Curaçaoan environment (Roberts and Manchester 2010: 174-176). Such infections may cause headache and unpleasant nasal discharge in modern populations (Edvardsson 2013, 509).

This individual also suffered from a variety of dental pathologies, which are informative about the type of food he was consuming. These included wear on the lingual (inside) surfaces of both maxillary first incisors (upper front teeth), known as LSAMAT or *lingual surface attrition of the maxillary anterior teeth* (Fricke & Laffoon, 2019). The presence of dental wear may be caused by the crowns of the teeth grinding against each other, or abrasion by a foreign object when the teeth are used as tools (Roberts and Manchester 2010: 78; Ortner 2003: 604; Pietrusewsky and Douglas 2002: 73-74). However, in the context of the Caribbean it is also possible that this type of wear was caused by eating acidic or sugary food such as sugarcane or manioc (Irish and Turner II 1997, 141-146). He also suffered from periodontal disease or infection of the gums, which can lead to ante-mortem tooth loss as the jaw bone recedes (Ogden 2008a, 285-309). Indeed, he lost several of his teeth before death. Additionally, calculus (mineralised dental plaque) was present at the gingival margin (gum line) (Fricke & Laffoon, 2019). Calculus has a complicated aetiology, but diets high in carbohydrate (such as sorghum) and poor oral hygiene are contributing factors in its development (Ogden 2008a, 285-309; Lieverse 1999, 219-232). Diets high in carbohydrates and sugars can also affect the enamel, causing cavities (carious lesions) to develop which can sometimes penetrate to the pulp chamber of the tooth and allow infections to develop (Hillson 2001, 249-289). In this case, a large carious lesion of the lower right second molar probably allowed infection to take hold, causing an abscess at the tooth root (Fricke & Laffoon, 2019). These form when infection of the pulp cavity necessitates the development of a sinus that will drain pus (Ogden 2008b).

These individuals remind us that the story of slavery does not stop in 1863, but continues past the 1970s when the paga tera system ended and into the present day, facilitating the use of early 20th century artefacts and skeletons in this study. Indeed, local populations are still dealing with its societal and political impacts (Haviser 2001), and the challenges faced by Indigenous Caribbean and African ancestry people under slavery and paga tera are still experienced by enslaved people all over the world, despite the fact that slavery is now illegal in most countries (Patterson 2012, 322-359).

***

The name *Curaçao* is thought to come from the Spanish word *corazon* (heart). Richenel Ansano has described the island as "a broken heart" in his article discussing how academics frequently neglect, dismiss, or downplay the important contribution of folk beliefs and practices to Curaçaoan culture and identity (Ansano 2006, 1-9). Indeed, one can see the island as a broken heart for many reasons. In my opinion, the biggest of these is the fact that emancipation is still unfinished. The experiences of enslaved people have left a mark on their descendants: not only the legacy of trauma, but also a vibrant culture, creativity, and resilience which make Curaçao one of the most diverse heritage contexts in the world. The data presented here give an insight not only into the mechanics of inequality, but also into the personal embodied lives of enslaved people, whose stories we can now tell for the first time.

REFERENCES

Abraham-van der Mark, E. 2001. "A Doomed Civilizing Offensive in Curacao, 1871-1875." In *History of Literature in the Caribbean, Volume 2*, edited by A. James, 625-631. Philadelphia: John Benjamins Publishing Company.

Akbar, N. 1996. *Breaking the Chains of Psychological Slavery*. Tallahassee, Florida: Mind Productions.

Albus, A. 2001. "For Oral to Written Literature: St Maarten, Saba, and St Eustatius." In *History of Literature in the Caribbean, Volume 2*, edited by A. James, 443-447. Philadelphia: John Benjamins Publishing Company.

Allen, R. 2017a. "Contesting Respectability and Sexual Politics in Post-Emancipation Curacao." In *Archaeologies of Erasures and Silences: Recovering Othered Languages, Literatures and Cultures in the Dutch Caribbean and Beyond, Volume 1*, edited by N. Faraclas, R. Severing, C. Weijer, E. Echteld, W. Rutgers and R. Dupey, 99-112. Curacao: University of Curacao.

———. 2014. "From Bondage to National Belonging in a Dutch Caribbean Context: Addressing the Yu Di Korsou in Post Emancipation Curacao, 1863-1915." In *Creole Connections: Transgressing Neocolonial Boundaries in the Languages, Literatures and Cultures on the ABC Islands and the Rest of the Dutch Caribbean*, edited by N. Faraclas, R. Severing, C. Weijer, E. Echteld and W. Rutgers, 39-56. Curacao: University of Curacao.

———. 2010. "Hende a Hasi Malu P'E: Popular Psychiatric Beliefs in Curacaoan Culture."Fundashon pa Planifikashon di Idioma and the Universiteit van de Nederlandse Antillen, .

———. 2007. *Di Ki Manera? A Social History of Afro-Curacaoans, 1863-1917*. Amsterdam: SWP Publishers.

———. 2012. "Music in Diasporic Context: The Case of Curacao and Intra-Caribbean Migration." *Black Music Research Journal* 32 (2): 51-65.

———. 2001. "Song Texts as Literature of Daily Life in the Netherlands Antilles." In *History of Literature in the Caribbean, Volume 2*, edited by A. James, 421-429. Philadelphia: John Benjamins Publishing Company.

———. 2017b. "Toward a More Representative Global History: The "Dutch" Caribbean Island of Curacao and the African Diaspora." In *Revisiting African Studies in a Globalized World*, edited by A. Awedoba, J. Gordon, E. Sutherland-Addy and A. Ampofo, 281-295. Legon: Smartline.

Anderson, W. and R. Dynes. 1975. *Social Movement, Violence and Change: The may Movement in Curacao*. Columbus: Ohio State University Press.

Ansano, R. 2006. "Living at the Edge of a Broken Heart." In *The Poetics of the Sacred and the Politics of Scholarship*, edited by T. Berger, 1-9. Duke University: The Worlds and Knowledges Otherwise.

Armstrong, D. and M. Fleischman. 2003. "House-Yard Burials of Enslaved Labourers in Eighteenth-Century Jamaica." *International Journal of Historical Archaeology* 7 (1): 33-65.

Bar-Anan, Y., T. Wilson, and D. Gilbert. 2009. "The Feeling of Uncertainty Intensifies Affective Reactions." *Emotion* 9 (1): 123-127.

Baron, J. 2009. "Sailors' Scurvy before and After James Lind – a Reassessment." *Nutrition Reviews* 67 (6): 315-332.

Battle-Baptiste, W. 2007. ""In this here Place": Interpreting Enslaved Homeplaces." In *Archaeology of the Atlantic Diaspora and the African Diaspora*, edited by A. Ogundiran and T. Falola, 233-248. Indianapolis: Indiana University Press.

———. 2011. *Black Feminist Archaeology*. Walnut Creek, California: Left Coast Press.

Blakey, M. and L. Rankin-Hill. 2009. *The New York African Burial Ground: Unearthing the African Presence in Colonial New York, Volume 1*. Washington DC: Howard University Press.

Blakey, M., L. Rankin-Hill, A. Goodman, and F. Jackson. 2009. "Discussion." In *Skeletal Biology of the New York Afrian Burial Ground, Part 1*, edited by M. Blakey and L. Rankin-Hill, 269-273. Washington D. C.: Howard University Press.

Blakey, M., L. Rankin-Hill, J. Howson, S. Wilson, and S. Carrington. 2009. "The Political Economy of Forced Migration: Sex Ratios, Mortality, Population Growth, and Fertility among Africans in Colonial New York." In *The New York African Burial Ground: Unearthing the African Presence in Colonial New York, Volume 1*, edited by M. Blakey and L. Rankin-Hill, 255-267. Washington DC: Howard University Press.

Brenneker, P. 2018. *Sambumbu: Volkskunde Van Curacao, Aruba En Bonaire. Mensen En Manieren*. Amsterdam: Caribpublishing.

———. 2017a. *Sambumbu: Volkskunde Van Curacao, Aruba En Bonaire. Religie En Rituelen*. Amsterdam: Caribpublishing.

———. 2017b. *Sambumbu: Volkskunde Van Curacao, Aruba En Bonaire. Zang En Muziek*. Amsterdam: Caribpublishing.

Broek, A. 2001. "Prewar Prose and Poetry in Papiamentu." In *History of Literature in the Caribbean, Volume 2*, edited by A. James, 633-641. Philadelphia: John Benjamins Publishing Company.

Broere, K. "Venezolaanse 'vreemdelingen' Kosten Curaçao Geld – En Zorgen Voor Onrust: 'Wij Willen Ons Geld, Nu!'." De Volkskrant, last modified February 28th, accessed June 22nd, 2019, https://www.volkskrant.nl/nieuws-achtergrond/venezolaanse-vreemdelingen-kosten-curacao-geld-en-zorgen-voor-onrust-wij-willen-ons-geld-nu~b2bbdc7a/.

Brothwell, D. 1981. *Digging Up Bones*. 3rd ed. London: Trustees of the British Museum.

Burnard, T. 2004. *Mastery, Tyranny, and Desire: Thomas Thistlewood and His Slaves in the Anglo-Jamaican World*. Chapel Hill: The University of North Carolina Press.

Carson, S. 2008. "The Effect of Geography and Vitamin D on African American Stature in the Nineteenth Century: Evidence from Prison Records." *Journal of Economic History* 68 (3): 812-831.

Craton, M. 2003 [1997]. "Slavery and Slave Society in the British Caribbean." In *The Slavery Reader*, edited by G. Heuman and J. Walvin, 103-111. Abingdon: Routledge.

Curacao Monuments. "Landhuis Veeris.", accessed August 17th, 2016, http://www.curacaomonuments.org/drov-information.php?geo_code=160100.

Dalphinis, M. 1985. *Caribbean and African Languages: Social History, Language, Literature and Education*. London: Karia Press.

Dandy, D. and D. Edwards. 2003. *Essential Orthopaedics and Trauma*. 4th ed. London: Churchill Livingstone.

de Palm, J., ed. 1985. *Encyclopedie Van De Nederlandse Antillen*. 2nd ed. Zutphen: De Walburg Pers.

Degloma, T. 2009. "Expanding Trauma through Space and Time: Mapping the Rhetorical Strategies of Trauma Carrier Groups." *Social Psychology Quarterly* 72 (2): 105-122.

DeWitte, S. and G. Hughes-Morey. 2012. "Stature and Frailty during the Black Death: The Effect of Stature on Risks of Epidemic Mortality in London, AD 1348-1350." *Journal of Archaeological Science* 39: 1412-1419.

Djuric-Srejic, M. and C. Roberts. 2001. "Palaeopathological Evidence of Infectious Disease in Skeletal Populations from Later Medieval Serbia." *International Journal of Osteoarchaeology* 11: 311-320.

do Rego, C. 2009. "Tula, Inspirado: De Vrijheidsidealen Van Een Curacaose Verzetstrijder." In *Tula: De Slavenopstand Van 1795 Op Curacao*, edited by A. Cain, 27-35. Amsterdam: NiNsee.

Douglass, F., ed. 2013. *Narrative of the Life of Frederick Douglass*: Amazon.

Dutch Caribbean Nature Alliance. "Queen Conch." Dutch Caribbean Nature Alliance, accessed June 22nd, 2019, https://www.dcnanature.org/queen-conch-2/.

Edvardsson, B. 2013. "Cluster Headache Associated with Acute Maxillary Sinusitis." *SpringerPlus* 2: 509.
Ellis, W. 1981. *Antilliana: Verzameld Werk Van Dr. W. Ch. De La Try Ellis*. Zutphen: De Walburg Pers.
Espersen, R. 2019. "From Hell's Gate to the Promised Land: Perspectives of Poverty in Saba, Dutch Caribbean, 1780 to Mid-20th Century." *Historical Archaeology* 53 (2).
Farris Thompson, R. 1990. "Kongo Influences on African-American Artistic Culture." In *Africanisms in American Culture*, edited by E. Holloway, 148-184. Indianapolis: Indiana University Press.
Fatah-Black, K. 2013. "Orangism, Patriotism, and Slavery in Curacao, 1795-1796." *International Review of Social History* 58: 35-60.
Finden-Crofts, J. 1998. "Calypso's Consequences." In *Material Cultures: Why some Things Matter*, edited by D. Miller, 147-166. London: UCL Press.
Finneran, N. 2016. "Slaves to Sailors: The Archaeology of Traditional Caribbean Shore Whaling C. 1850-2000: A Case Study from Barbados and Bequia (St Vincent Grenadines)." *International Journal of Nautical Archaeology* 45 (2): 388-405.
Fouse, G. 2002. *The Story of Papiamentu: A Study in Slavery and Language*. Oxford: University Press of America.
Franklin, M. 2017. *Archaeology and Enslaved Life on Coke's Plantation: An Early History of the Governor's Palace Lands*. Virginia: The Colonial Williamsburg Foundation.
Fricke, F., J. Laffoon, A. Victorina, and J. Haviser. 2019. Delayed physical development in a first generation enslaved African woman from Pietermaai, Curacao. *International Journal of Osteoarchaeology* 30 (1): 43-52.
Gibbes, F., N. Romer-Kenepa, and M. Scriwanek. 2015. *De Curacaoenaar in De Geschiedenis 1499-2010*. Willemstad: Stichting Nationale Geschiedenis.
Given, M. 2004. *The Archaeology of the Colonized*. London: Routledge.
Goode-Null, S., K. Shujaa, and L. Rankin-Hill. 2009. "Subadult Growth and Development." In *Skeletal Biology of the New York Afrian Burial Ground, Part 1*, edited by M. Blakey and L. Rankin-Hill, 227-253. Washington D. C.: Howard University Press.
Goslinga, C. 1979. *A Short History of the Netherlands Antilles and Suriname*. Den Haag: Martinus Nijhoff.
Goveia, E. 1991 [1960]. "The West Indian Slave Laws of the Eighteenth Century." In *Caribbean Slave Society and Economy: A Student Reader*, edited by H. Beckles and V. Shepherd, 346-362. London: James Currey.
Gowland, R. 2016. "Elder Abuse: Evaluating the Potentials and Problems of Diagnosis in the Archaeological Record." *International Journal of Osteoarchaeology* 26 (3): 514-523.
Guerreiro Ramos Bennett, E. 1999. "Gabriella Cravo E Canela: Jorge Amado and the Myth of the Sexual Mulata in Brazilian Culture." In *The African Diaspora: African Origins and New World Identities*, edited by I. Okpewho, C. Boyce Davies and A. Mazrui, 227-233. Indianapolis: Indiana University Press.
Hamilakis, Y. 2016. "Archaeologies of Forced and Undocumented Migration." *Journal of Contemporary Archaeology* 3 (2): 121-139.
Haviser, J. 1995. *An AAINA Project Proposal for the Archaeological Study of Community Development in the Vicinity of Landhuis Knip, Curacao*. Curacao: Archaeological-Anthropological Institute of the Netherlands Antilles (AAINA).
———. 2001. "Emancipation as a Continuing Process." In *Freedom in Black History and Culture*, edited by E. Kofi Agorsah. Portland, Oregon: Arrow Press.
———. 1999. "Identifying a Post-Emancipation (1863-1940) African-Curacaoan Material Culture Assemblage." In *African Sites Archaeology of the Caribbean*, edited by J. Haviser, 221-263. Jamaica: Ian Randle Publishers.

———. 1993. *Observation of Human Skeletal Remains by the Archaeological-Anthropological Institute of the Netherands Antilles, October 6, 1993, Police Report*. Curacao: Archaeological-Anthropological Institute of the Netherlands Antilles (AAINA).

Higman, B. 1979. "Growth in Afro-Caribbean Slave Populations." *American Journal of Physical Anthropology* 50: 373-386.

Hillson, S. 2001. "Recording Dental Caries in Archaeological Human Remains." *International Journal of Osteoarchaeology* 11: 249-289.

Hoonhout, B. and T. Mareite. 2018. "Freedom at the Fringes? Slave Flight and Empire-Building in the Early Modern Spanish Borderlands of Essequibo-Venezuela and Louisiana-Texas." *Slavery and Abolition* 40 (1): 61-86.

Huijers, D. and L. Ezechiels. 1992. *Landhuizen Van Curacao En Bonaire*. Amsterdam: Uitgeverij Persimmons Management BV.

Infomistico. "Virgen Del Valle: Historia Y Milagros De La Virgen Del Valle." WordPress, last modified September 8, accessed May 27, 2019, https://www.infomistico.com/portal/virgen-del-valle/.

Irish, J. and C. Turner II. 1997. "Brief Communication: First Evidence of LSAMAT in Non-Native Americans: Historica Senegalese from West Africa." *American Journal of Physical Anthropology* 102: 141-146.

JanMohamed, A. 2010. "Between Speaking and Dying: Some Imperatives in the Emergence of the Subaltern in the Context of US Slavery." In *Can the Subaltern Speak? Reflections on the History of an Idea*, edited by R. Morris, 139-155. New York: Columbia University Press.

JanMohamed, A. 2005. *The Death-Bound-Subject: Richard Wright's Archaeology of Death*. London: Duke University Press.

Jordaan, H. 2003. "The Curacao Slave Market: From Asiento Trade to Free Trade, 1700-1730." In *Riches from Atlantic Commerce: Transatlantic Slave Trade and Shipping, 1585-1817*, edited by J. Postma and V. Enthoven, 219-257. Leiden: Brill.

———. 2013. *Slavernij En Vrijheid Op Curacao: De Dynamiek Van Een Achttiende-Eeuws Atlantisch Handelsknooppunt*. Zutphen: Walburg Pers.

Jurmain, R., F. Cardoso, C. Henderson, and S. Villotte. 2012. "Bioarchaeology's Holy Grail: The Reconstruction of Activity." In *A Companion to Palaeopathology*, edited by A. Grauer, 531-552. Chichester: John Wiley and Sons Ltd.

Kamash, Z. 2008. "What Lies Beneath? Perceptions of the Ontological Paradox of Water." *World Archaeology* 40 (2): 224-237.

Kas di Kultura. "From Country-House Kenepa to Tula Museum." Kas di Kultura, accessed August/03, 2016, www.museotula.com.

Kessler, J., H. Nikizad, K. Shea, J. Jacobs, J. Bebchuk, and J. Weiss. 2014. "The Demographics and Epidemiology of Osteochondritis Dissecans of the Knee in Children and Adolescents." *American Journal of Sports Medicine* 42: 320-326.

Kiple, K. and V. Kiple. 1991 [1980]. "Deficiency Diseases in the Caribbean." In *Caribbean Slave Society and Economy: A Student Reader*, edited by H. Beckles and V. Shepherd, 173-182. London: James Currey.

Laffoon, J., T. Sonneman, T. Shafie, C. Hofman, U. Brandes, and G. Davies. 2017. "Investigating Human Geographic Origins using Dual-Isotope (87Sr/86Sr/d18O) Assignment Approaches." *PLOS One* 12 (2).

Lampe, A. 2001. "Christianity and Slavery in the Dutch Caribbean." In *Christianity in the Caribbean: Essays on Church History*, edited by A. Lampe, 126-153. Barbados: University of the West Indies.

Langenfeld, E. 2007. *Verhalen Uit Het Verleden*. Curacao: Drukkerij de Curacaosche Courant.

―――. 2010. *Verhalen Uit Het Verleden. Deel 2.* Curacao: Drukkerij de Curacaosche Courant.
Lewis, G. 1983. *Main Currents in Caribbean Thought: The Historical Evolution of Caribbean Society in its Ideological Aspects, 1492-1900.* London: The John Hopkins University Press.
Lieverse, A. 1999. "Diet and the Aetiology of Dental Calculus." *International Journal of Osteoarchaeology* 9: 219-232.
Lima, T., M. de Souza, and G. Sene. 2014. "Weaving the Second Skin: Protection Against Evil among the Valongo Slaves in Nineteenth-Century Rio De Janeiro." *Journal of African Diaspora Archaeology and Heritage* 3 (2): 103-136.
Madrigal, L. 2006. *Human Biology of Afro-Caribbean Populations.* Cambridge: Cambridge University Press.
Marcha, V. and P. Verweel. 2003. *De Cultuur Van Angst.* Amsterdam: Uitgeverij SWP.
Marcha, V., P. Verweel, and J. Werkman. 2012. *Kleur Bekennen: Idealisering En Ontkenning Van De Eigen Huidskleur.* Amsterdam: Caribpublishing/BV Uitgeverij SWP.
Margo, R. and R. Steckel. 1982. "The Heights of American Slaves: New Evidence on Slave Nutrition and Health." *Social Science History* 6 (4): 516-538.
Martinus, F. 1997. "The Kiss of a Slave: Papiamentu's West African Connections. PhD Thesis."University of Amsterdam.
Mays, S., J. Steele, and M. Ford. 1999. "Direcitonal Asymmetry in the Human Clavicle." *International Journal of Osteoarchaeology* 9: 18-28.
Merrill, J. and S. Thomas. 2013. "Interactions between Adaptive Coping and Drinking to Cope in Predicting Naturalistic Drinking and Drinking Following a Lab-Based Psychosocial Stressor." *Addictive Behaviour* 38 (3): 1672-1678.
Miller, J. and R. Miller. 1987. "Jeremy Bentham's Panoptic Device." *October* 41: 3-29.
Moshenska, G. and A. Gonzalez-Ruibal. 2015. "Introduction: The Only Way is Ethics." In *Ethics and the Archaeology of Violence. Ethical Archaeologies: The Politics of Social Justice 2*, edited by A. Gonzalez-Ruibal and G. Moshenska, 1-17. New York: Springer.
Odewale, A. and M. Hardy 2019. "Royal Enslaved Afro-Caribbeans in Christiansted: Exploring the Archaeology of Enslavement in a Caribbean City." In *Archaeology of Domestic Landscapes of the Enslaved in the Caribbean*, edited by Delle, J. and E. Clay, 188-216. Gainesville: University of Florida Press.
Ogden, A. 2008a. "Advances in the Palaeopathology of Teeth and Jaws." In *Advances in Human Palaeopathology*, edited by R. Pinhasi and S. Mays, 285-309. London: John Wiley and Sons Ltd.
―――. 2008b. "Periapical Voids in Human Jaw Bones." In Smith, M. and Brickley, M. (Eds.). Proceedings of the Eighth Annual Conference of the British Association for Biological Anthropology and Osteoarchaeology. Oxford: Archaeopress. British Archaeological Reports International Series 1743. pp.51-56.
Ogundiran, A. 2002. "Of Small Things Remembered: Beads, Cowries, and Cultural Transitions of the Atlantic." *The International Journal of African Historical Studies* 35 (2/3): 427-457.
Ono-George, M. 2017. "'By Her Unnatural and Despicable Conduct': Motherhood and Concubinage in the Watchman and Jamaica Free Press, 1830-1833." *Slavery and Abolition* 38 (2): 356-372.
Oostindie, G. 2005. *Paradise Overseas: The Dutch Caribbean: Colonialism and its Transatlantics Legacies.* Oxford: Macmillan Caribbean.
―――. 1995. "Same Old Song? Perspectives on Slavery and Slaves in Suriname and Curacao." In *Fifty Years Later: Antislavery, Capitalism and Modernity in the Dutch Orbit*, edited by G. Oostindie, 143-178. Leiden: KITLV Press.

———. 2011. "Slave Resistance, Colour Lines, and the Impact of the French and Haitian Revolutions in Curacao." In *Curacao in the Age of Revolutions, 1795-1800*, edited by W. Klooster and G. Oostindie, 1-22. Leiden: KITLV Press.
Ortner, D. 2003. *Identification of Pathological Conditions in Human Skeletal Remains*. 2nd ed. London: Academic Press.
Ousley, S. and R. Jantz. 2005. *FORDISC 3.0: Personal Computer Forensic Discriminant Functions*. Knoxville: University of Tennessee.
Oyewumi, O. 2006 [1997]. "Colonizing Bodies and Minds." In *The Post-Colonial Studies Reader*, edited by B. Ashcroft, G. Griffiths and H. Tiffin. 2nd ed., 256-259. London: Routledge.
Patterson, O. 1982. *Slavery and Social Death: A Comparative Study*. London: Harvard University Press.
———. 2012. "Trafficking, Gender and Slavery: Past and Present." In *The Legal Understanding of Slavery: From the Historical to the Contemporary*, edited by J. Allain, 322-359. Oxford: Oxford University Press.
Paula, A. 1968. *From Objective to Subjective Social Barriers: A Historico-Philiosophical Analysis of Certain Negative Attitudes among the Negroid Population of Curacao*. Curacao: Drukkerij De Curacaosche Courant.
———. 1987. *Slavery in a Nutshell* Central Historical Archives.
Pietrusewsky, M. and M. Douglas. 2002. *Ban Chiang, A Prehistoric Village Site in Northeast Thailand, Volume 1: The Human Skeletal Remains*. Pennsylvania: University of Pennsylvania Press.
Ponce, P. 2012. "A Comparative Study of Markers of Occupational Stress in Coastal Fishers and Inland Agriculturalists from Northern Chile." In *Proceedings of the Twelfth Annual Conference of the British Association for Biological Anthropology and Osteoarchaeology. BAR International Series 2380*, edited by P. Mitchell and J. Buckberry, 71-85. Oxford: Hadrian Books Ltd.
Prince, M. 2008. *The History of Mary Prince, A West Indian Slave*. Radford: Wilder Publications LLC.
Prost, S., C. Lemieux, and A. Ai. 2016. "Social Work Students in the Aftermath of Hurricanes Katrina and Rita: Correlates of Post-Disaster Substance use as a Negatives Coping Mechanism." *Social Work Education* 35 (7): 825-844.
Redactie. "Venezuela Sluit Zich Af Van Aruba, Bonaire En Curaçao." De Volkskrant, last modified February 20th, accessed June 22nd, 2019, https://www.volkskrant.nl/nieuws-achtergrond/venezuela-sluit-zich-af-van-aruba-bonaire-en-curacao~b13fe571/.
Roberts, C. and K. Manchester. 2010. *The Archaeology of Disease*. 3rd ed. Gloucester: Sutton Publishing.
Roe, A. 2016. "The Sound of Silence: Ideology of National Identity and Racial Inequality in Contemporary Curacao." PhD, Florida International University.
Roitman, J. 2017. ""A Mass of Mestiezen, Castiezen, and Mulatten": Contending with Color in the Netherlands Antilles, 1750-1850." *Atlantic Studies* 14 (3): 399-417.
Rosalia, R. 1997. "Tambu: De Legale En Kerkelijke Repressie Van Afro-Curacaose Volksuitingen. PhD Thesis."University of Amsterdam.
Rupert, L. 2012. *Creolization and Contraband: Curacao in the Early Modern Atlantic World*. London: University of Georgia Press.
Schiltkamp, J., B. Smit, and S. Wachlin. 2000. *Soublette et Fils: Photography in Curacao Around 1900*. Amsterdam: KIT Publishers.
Slavernij en Jij. "Woordgebruik Verantwoording." Eagerly Internet, accessed June 22nd, 2019, https://www.slavernijenjij.nl/verantwoording-woordgebruik/.
Smith-Guzman, N. 2015. "The Skeletal Manifestation of Malaria: An Epidemiological Approach using Documented Skeletal Collections." *American Journal of Physical Anthropology* 158: 624-635.

Snoddy, A., H. Buckley, G. Elliott, V. Standen, B. Arriaza, and S. Halcrow. 2018. "Macroscopic Features of Scurvy in Human Skeletal Remains: A Literature Synthesis and Diagnostic Guide." *American Journal of Physical Anthropology* July: 1-20.
Spangler, D. 2010. "Heavenly Bodies: Religious Issues in Cognitive Behavioural Treatment of Eating Disorders." *Cognitive and Behavioural Practice* 17: 358-370.
Stone, R. and J. Stone. 2009. *Atlas of the Skeletal Muscles*. 7th ed. New York: McGraw-Hill.
Sule, E., R. Sutton, D. Jones, I. Igbo, and L. Jones. 2017. "The Past does Matter: A Nursing Perspective on Post Traumatic Slave Syndrone (PTSS)." *Journal of Racial and Ethnic Health Disparities* 4: 779-783.
Swift, E. 2012. "Object Biography, Re-use and Recycling in the Late to Post-Roman Period and Beyond: Rings made from Romano-British Bracelets." *Britannia* 43: 167-215.
Sypkens-Smit, M. 1981. *Rapport Ter Voorlopige Afsluiting Van Het Cultureel Antropologisch Onderzoek on Sint Maarten (NA)*. Leiden: Koninklijk Instituut Taal- Land- en Volkenkunde (KITLV).
Teaford, M. and J. Lytle. 1996. "Brief Communication: Diet-Induced Changes in Rates of Human Tooth Microwear: A Case Study Involving Stone-Ground Maize." *American Journal of Physical Anthropology* 100 (1): 143-147.
Thomas, D. 2016. "Time and the Otherwise: Plantations, Garrisons and being Human in the Caribbean." *Anthropological Theory* 16 (2-3): 177-200.
Thomas, H. 1997. *The Slave Trade: The History of the Atlantic Slave Trade 1440-1870*. London: Orion Books Ltd.
van der Dijs, N. 2011. "The Nature of Ethnic Identity among the People of Curacao. PhD Thesis."Koninklijk Instituut voor Taal- Land- en Volkenkunde (KITLV).
van der Ven, C. 2011. *Slagschaduwen: Erfenis Van Een Koloniaal Verleden*. Amsterdam: KIT Publishers.
Veeris, D. "Dinah's Favorieten.", accessed October 18th, 2017, https://www.dinah veeris.com/dinah_favorieten.html.
Victorina, A. and C. Kraan. 2012. *Vondsten Uit De Bodem Van Fleur De Marie Te Curacao: Een Archeologisch Bureau - En Inventariserend Veldonderzoek*. Curacao: National Archaeological Anthropological Memory Management (NAAM).
Villotte, S. and C. Knusel. 2014. ""I Sing of Arms and of the Man…": Medial Epicondylosis and the Sexual Division of Labour in Prehistoric Europe." *Journal of Archaeological Science* 43: 168-174.
Vlach, J. 1976a. "Affecting Architecture of the Yoruba." *African Arts* 10 (1): 48-53.
———. 1976b. "The Shotgun House: An African Architectural Legacy, Part II." *Pioneer America* 8 (2): 57-70.
Waldron, T. 1997. "Osteoarthritis of the Hip in Past Populations." *International Journal of Osteoarchaeology* 7: 186-189.
Walker, P. 1997. "Wife Beating, Boxing, and Broken Noses: Skeletal Evidence for the Cultural Patterning of Violence." In *Troubled Times: Violence and Warfare in the Past*, edited by D. Martin and D. Frayer, 145-179. UK: Gordon and Breach Publishers.
Walker, P., R. Bathurst, R. Richman, T. Gjerdrum, and V. Andrushko. 2009. "The Causes of Porotic Hyperostosis and Cribra Orbitalia: A Reappraisal of the Iron-Deficiency-Anemia Hypothesis." *American Journal of Physical Anthropology* 139: 109-125.
Wallman, D. 2014. "Slave Community Foodways on a French Colonial Plantation: Zooarchaeology at Habitation Creve Coeur, Marinique." In *Bitasion: Lesser Antilles Plantation Archaeology*, edited by K. Kelly and B. Berard, 45-68. Leiden: Sidestone Academic Press.
Werbata, J.V.D. 1906. *Topographische kaart van Curaçao*. Nederlandse Cartografische Dienst. Den Haag: Smulders & Co.

Wilkie, L. 1997. "Secret and Sacred: Contextualizing the Artifacts of African-American Magic and Religion." *Historical Archaeology* 31 (4): 81-106.
Wilson, D. 1995. "The Analysis of Domestic Reuse in Historical Archaeology." In *Expanding Archaeology*, edited by J. Skibo, W. Walker and A. Nielsen, 126-140. Salt Lake City: University of Utah Press.
Winkel, P. 1987. *Scharloo, a Nineteenth Century Quarter of Willemstad, Curacao: Historical Architecture and its Background*. Florence: Edizioni Pligrafico Florentino.

CHAPTER 3

St. Eustatius: A Golden Rock

Figure 3.1: Map of St Eustatius showing key sites: Scotsenhoek Plantation, Fair Play Plantation, Witten Hoek, the Lazaretto, Fort Amsterdam, and Oranjestad.

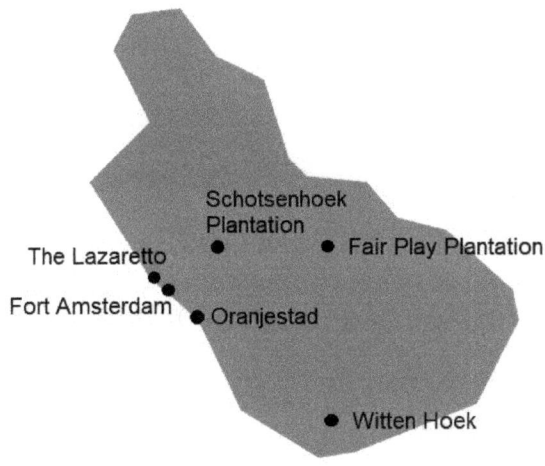

Source: Pepijn van der Linden and Felicia J Fricke.

A CHINESE GARDEN

Figure 3.2: Fragment of Delftware found at Fair Play Plantation.

Source: Felicia J. Fricke.

This piece of blue-and-white pottery from Fair Play Plantation on St Eustatius shows a rich European family walking through a Chinese garden. Its style is representative of the Dutch Delftware tradition, which was influenced by designs originally imported from China, and which therefore often reflected an interaction between the familiar and the 'exotic' (Odell 2010, 141-158). Another piece of blue-and-white Delftware dated 1630 to 1790 and on display in the St Eustatius Historical Foundation Museum shows a windmill (which would have been very familiar to the Dutch colonisers of St Eustatius) in a flat landscape, with trees that may be oaks or elms, birds in the sky, and the words *Bring More Cane to Mill Negro* underneath. This is an interesting juxtaposition of European and Caribbean imagery that might not have seemed dissonant to the inhabitants of St Eustatius. The most important contribution of representations like these ones is psychological. They are able to tell us something about the way that both slave owners and enslaved people lived their lives.

Fair Play Plantation is located in the fertile middle region of St Eustatius, and was one of the largest sugar plantations on the island (Cook and Stelten 2014). Map evidence shows that it was in productive use from the early to mid-18th century and completely abandoned by 1915 (Cook 2015). The status of the island as a free port (the 18th century equivalent of a tax haven) from 1754 onwards meant that sugar producers from the surrounding British islands (particularly Jamaica, St Kitt's, and Nevis) could make a higher profit processing their sugar at Fair Play and other Statian plantations than they could at home (Gilmore III and Nelson 2015, 305-334). Statians came to make much more money in trade and exchange than in the production of cash crops (such as tobacco, cotton, coffee, and indigo, see EUX-OH-01; EUX-OH-02; EUX-OH-04) because of the low annual rainfall and frequent drought (Barka 2001, 82-92). The island became known as 'the Golden Rock' because of its commercial success, and by the end of the 18th century the narrow strip of Oranjestad between the cliff and the sea had been filled with over 600 buildings, many of them warehouses (Gilmore III and Nelson 2015, 305-334). In 1775 a Scottish lady called Janet Schaw arrived in Oranjestad and wrote:

> From one end of the town to the other is a continued mart, where goods of the most different uses and qualities are displayed before the shop-doors. Here hang rich embroideries, painted silks, flowered Muslins, with all the Manufactures of the Indies... I bought a quantity of excellent French gloves for fourteen pence a pair, also English thread-stockings cheaper than I could buy them at home. *(Schaw 1921: 137-138)*

Because of this commercial focus, most enslaved people were employed in shipbuilding and trade activities, rather than on the plantations (Gilmore III 2006a, 70-89: 87). The minor economic role of cash crop production meant that the plantations came to fill a role not unlike that of the country estate, and were important expressions of social status (Gilmore III and Nelson 2015, 305-334). The elite culture of the island revolved around the flamboyant display of material wealth, as was common across the Caribbean (Stelten 2013).

The Fair Play enslaved village excavated by the St Eustatius Centre for Archaeological Research (SECAR) was occupied during the late 18th to early 19th centuries (Cook and Stelten 2014: 32). It is located next to a stone building which may have been the overseer's house, so that enslaved people felt that they were constantly observed (Gilmore III 2005: 290). This makes Fair Play something of a Statian anomaly: most of the other plantations on the island have enslaved villages which are located out of sight of the owners and overseers (Stelten 2013). Various authors have suggested that enslaved people in Statia therefore had increased freedom of movement and privacy of domestic life, when compared to other islands (Stelten 2013; Gilmore III 2005: 291).

Archaeologists identified four post-in-ground wooden house structures and two fences in the excavated area. Extra post-holes indicated that the houses were remodelled over time, but they all conform to a single alignment, so the settlement was probably pre-planned rather than being allowed to grow organically. The artefacts recovered were mostly from post-hole fills relating to the early 19th century phase of the site, around the time of abandonment, although some artefacts came from pits that were filled earlier in the period of habitation (Cook and Stelten 2014). There was a variety of European imported ceramics and glass (including beautiful drinking vessels) which were more widely available and cheaper on St Eustatius than they were on other islands (Schaw 1921: 137-138). We know from his autobiographical narrative that the enslaved sailor Olaudah Equiano was able to trade glassware and livestock in Oranjestad during his brief visit to the island in the 18th century (Equiano 1999 [1814]: 78), and this is also reflected in the island's oral history:

> EUX-OH-01: ... it was so prospering here that sometimes too that slaves were even able, some of them were lucky enough to move up through the ranks in obtaining a piece of land. They would also manage slaves or be head over slaves. And some of them even owned like little shops and did little trade among themselves [...] it will most likely be shops maybe with selling little provisions or probably sugar or like little knickknacks.

Indeed, some freed people even chose to stay on St Eustatius and take advantage of its economic opportunities (Gilmore III 2010, 43-53). In the St Eustatius Historical Foundation Museum there is a gravestone with the name *Cwan Pedro* (probably Juan Pedro, a Portuguese name) inscribed upon it. A freedman at the time of his death, Juan Pedro owned one of these little shops (EUX-OH-01). Analysis of pottery from St Eustatius has also indicated that enslaved people probably produced their own ceramics and sold them to people on nearby islands, for example Antigua and Nevis. Likewise, pottery from Nevis and St Croix has been found on St Eustatius, indicating that there was two-way exchange (Gilmore III 2005: 133-134). These locally made earthenwares are built up by hand (rather than thrown on a wheel), unglazed, fired without a kiln, and probably indicate a syncretic interaction between West and Central African and European ceramic traditions in a Caribbean environment (Heath 1999, 196-220). Flat-bottomed vessels, for example, may demonstrate European influences, while round-bottomed vessels designed to be balanced on fire stones are more African (Gilmore III 2005: 140). Some types of ceramic recorded on St Eustatius could indeed have been used for cooking over an open fire, and the assemblages also include bowl, plate, and storage jar fragments. The study of Afro-Caribbean pottery has in general been very important in the investigation of creolisation and enslaved lifeways because it is the only type of object manufactured by enslaved people that consistently survives well in archaeology (Hauser 2011, 431-447), and this exchange between and among enslaved communities is sometimes described as a 'proto-peasant economy' (see Craton 2003 [1997], 103-111). It demonstrates the inability of slave owners to completely control all aspects of the enslaved people's lives.

As mentioned above, historical sources tell us that enslaved people on St Eustatius may have been afforded a degree of 'freedom' seldom seen elsewhere (Gilmore III 2006a, 70-89). In Oranjestad, enslaved people often lived separately from their masters (Heath 1999, 196-220). The roles that they played as coopers, distillers, barbers, and sailors allowed some to earn their manumission more quickly than enslaved people on other islands (EUX-OH-10; Gilmore III 2010, 43-53). St Eustatius' small size meant that runaways did not really have anywhere to go, and owners may not therefore have felt the need to maintain constant supervision (Stelten 2013). This encouraged greater freedom of movement for enslaved people (Gilmore

III 2006a, 70-89). Richard Grant Gilmore III's documentary research on advertisements for the return of runaways even implies that some enslaved people here could read, and that slave owners were aware of this fact (Gilmore III 2006a, 70-89), although it possible that these adverts were intended to be read *to* the enslaved person rather than *by* them. Literacy could be an act of resistance for enslaved people:

> EUX-OH-01: if you were caught that even make a markings on the ground, even in the dirt and it comes up looking like an alphabetical letter you will be severely beaten and punished.

As in Curaçao, there was a division between enslaved people employed in the domestic arena and those who worked in the fields. These divisions and fractures fostered resentment, prevented unity, and made it less likely that communities would be able to organise escape and revolt (Lewis 1983).

> EUX-OH-01: that is where the difference, some of them felt they were better than the other slaves. Because they were treated differently, they were dressed differently, *et cetera*. But still they were a slave, whichever way you put it.

Other psychological hardships included being treated like a perpetual minor or ridiculous, ugly, or inferior being:

> EUX-OH-01: And also some of the masters used to watch the slaves entertaining themselves for recreation [...] they think it's funny [...] if you are a child or you are adult you still be treated as a child, you are told what to do, you are treated less than an animal [...] you will be ridiculed for your own colour, your skin.

The loss of personal identity ("when you come from Africa no one will know what your last name was. [...] You get a new name." EUX-OH-01) and constant stress and uncertainty (for example the fear that families would be broken up when the slave owner decided to sell) also put pressure on enslaved people (EUX-OH-01; EUX-OH-06). Enslaved people might try and cultivate a good relationship with their master in the hope of receiving rewards such as food and status, but this was a dangerous strategy because it was such an unequal relationship (EUX-OH-01). Interviewees observed that these circumstances are still affecting people in St Eustatius today:

> EUX-OH-02: we're scared to take risks and do things because we are looking for the master non-stop to tell us what to do, and I think that in that sense in that dynamic yes it still exists and we call that one the 'mental slavery' where you still act as your ancestors.

Slaafgemaackt: Rethinking Enslavement in the Dutch Caribbean

I have already discussed in Chapter 2 how psychologists are taking these inherited effects seriously, addressing them under such terms as Post Traumatic Slave Syndrome (Sule et al. 2017, 779-783). Indeed, sociologists and anthropologists have often noted social dynamics on the island which relate to its history (Leslie 2018; van den Bor 1981: 18, 395, 399). In this context, the ceramic fragment described above demonstrates how the upper classes on the island saw the enslaved people: firstly, referring to them as *Negro*, thereby reinforcing the racial divide between free and unfree; and secondly, the fact that this harsh, demanding sentence ("Bring more cane to mill, Negro!") was normalised to the point where it decorated a piece of tableware.

FORT AMSTERDAM

Below is the skull of a woman of African ancestry rescued from a Statian cliff edge to the north of Oranjestad. Since 2012, archaeologists from SECAR and a team from Texas State University have been recovering human remains from this location before they are lost to the sea. The fragile sandy cliff is very vulnerable to erosion: perhaps half of the burial ground has already been lost (Morsink 2012). It is just one of hundreds of sites across the Caribbean which will become ever more vulnerable to damage with the more frequent hurricanes caused by global warming.

The burial ground is located next to Fort Amsterdam, which was constructed as a battery (or gun emplacement) constructed on a natural rise in the late 17th century, and was intended to protect the Oranje Bay with cannon fire (Hartog 1997: 130-133). It was one of twenty-four fortifications built on the island during the 17th and 18th centuries (Hartog 1997). However, even the large Fort Oranje on the Oranjestad clifftop was unfit for purpose, seldom saw any real conflict, and was more effective as a symbol of prosperity (Gilmore III and Roth 2013, 76-91). The Netherlands relied instead on neutrality to protect its colonies (Oostindie and Roitman 2012). Despite this strategy, the island was passed between the French, Dutch and English twenty-two times between 1629 and 1816, after which it became permanently Dutch (Karklins and Barka 1989, 55-80). St Eustatius was a desirable possession because of its sheltered harbour and favourable location in relation to Caribbean trade routes (Gilmore III and Nelson 2015, 305-334).

Fort Amsterdam fell out of use as a battery during the French and English occupations of the late 17th and early 18th centuries. In the 1720s, when the Dutch returned to the island, it became a depot which held enslaved people awaiting sale. With only a 16.4 x 6.4m ground plan, the building nevertheless held over 400 people at a time. Defensive qualities of the location now prevented escape (Hartog 1997: 130-133). By 1725, two to three thousand enslaved people came through this building each year, and were sold on to the French, English, and Spanish colonies (Cook and Stelten 2014; Emmer 2011, 450-475). In 1742 an extra storey was added to the fort building so that more people could be accommodated (Gilmore III 2006b, 83-96). The individuals buried nearby may therefore have been prisoners from the depot, or alternatively they may have been enslaved on one of the neighbouring plantations (such as Godet, which is only a short walk along the coastline) and buried in this location out of convenience. A document from 1738 does mention that individuals of African ancestry were buried on the sea front close to the manchineel trees (which were still there when I visited in 2017, their poisons burning the skin from passers-by just as they had done 300 years before) (Knappert 1932: 37).

Figure 3.3: The skull of a woman buried at Fort Amsterdam in the 18th century.

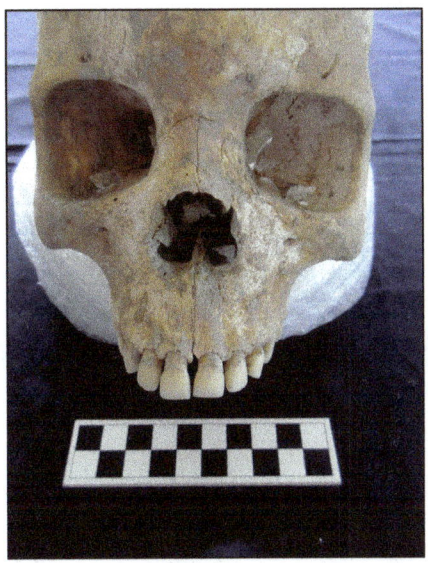

Source: Felicia J. Fricke.

One of the buried individuals was an adult probably of Indigenous descent according to both morphological analysis and to the computer program FORDISC 3.0 (which I mentioned in Chapter 2). Because the comparative database that FORDISC 3.0 uses is not exhaustive (in fact containing no Indigenous insular Caribbean populations at all) I must apply a certain amount of circumspection when I look at the results. In the case of this individual, the computer program determined that (s)he was most metrically similar to American Indian Females or Guatemalan Males. This result indicated to me that the individual was probably of Indigenous ancestry, because Indigenous populations of the insular Caribbean are more metrically similar to Indigenous North American and Guatemalan populations than they are to African or European populations. (Unfortunately, the skeletal elements that could have helped untangle this mystery further – the teeth and much of the facial region – were missing.) The original inhabitants of St Eustatius, who had lived on the island from at least the 7th to 9th century AD, were Arawak speakers and part of the Taíno ethnic group. However, they had left the island before the French first arrived in 1629 (Haviser 2001, 60-81). The early European inhabitants of St Eustatius therefore experimented with the use of kidnapped Indigenous Dominicans as enslaved labourers (Hartog 1976: 21) and the first enslaved Africans were brought to St Eustatius in the 1640s to work on the plantations (Haviser 2001, 60-81). By 1650 they had completely replaced the Indigenous enslaved people and by 1750 they outnumbered the Europeans 2:1 (Crane 1999: xiv; Heath 1999, 196-220). This Indigenous ancestry individual does not therefore represent the original population of the island, but rather a movement of people between Caribbean islands. It is possible that this individual was involved in the life of the depot, port, or nearby plantations in some way without being a member of the enslaved population, for example by being a sailor, although creole enslaved people traded within the Caribbean could have European and Indigenous Caribbean as well as African ancestry (MacEachern 2011, 34-57; Blakely 1993: 6).

Other individuals buried here include two infants, and two young or middle adult women, one of whom suffered from LSAMAT like the individual mentioned in Chapter 2. Younger women are more likely to have fallen within the demographic desired by buyers in the Caribbean, who preferred them for domestic tasks (Madrigal 2006: 30). Additionally, a man of African ancestry excavated by the island archaeologist in 2019 has a very interesting pathology: he appears to have survived a fracture to his first cervical vertebra (atlas). This is the vertebra just below the skull, and together with the second cervical vertebra (which acts as a kind of pivot) it allows movement of the head from side to side. In modern populations, fractures to the atlas are often caused by sporting accidents and managed with immobilisation or surgery. Immobilisation is a lot less effective than surgery and can lead to non-union of the broken pieces and persistent neck pain. There is also the potential for more serious neurological damage if the broken bone puts pressure on the spinal cord (Kim and Shim 2019, 685-693). In the case of the man buried at Fort Amsterdam, a false joint (pseudoarthrosis) has formed between the broken pieces at the back of the first cervical vertebra. This is not unexpected given that even immobilisation was probably not available to him. The fracture probably caused him neck problems for the rest of his life.

The presence of both Indigenous Caribbean and African ancestry individuals at the Fort Amsterdam burial ground is physical evidence of the diversity of Statian population during this time period. Indeed, St Eustatius was a "melting pot" (EUX-OH-01) of different cultures and therefore a nexus of communication. Interviewees mentioned those of English (EUX-OH-03), Dutch, Danish (EUX-OH-02), and Indigenous Caribbean (EUX-OH-05) descent, and documentary resources also state that the island hosted people from all over the world (Schaw 1921: 137-138). The WIC itself employed people of many different nationalities (Blakely 1993: 4). That English came to be adopted as the dominant language in St Eustatius was itself a mark of the island's cosmopolitan environment (Haviser 2001, 60-81).

...never did I meet with such variety; here was a merch[an]t vending his goods in Dutch, another in French, a third in Spanish... the diversity is really amusing. (Schaw 1921: 137-138)

By the end of the 18[th] century, the trade in enslaved people had abandoned St Eustatius as an important nodal point (Hartog 1997: 130-133). It was outlawed in 1784 and the economic fortunes of the island thereafter declined (Barka 2001, 82-92; Haviser 2001, 60-81; Karklins and Barka 1989, 55-80). Before we discuss this decline further, however, we should pursue further the economic highs of Statian commerce and how they might (or might not) have affected enslaved lifeways.

PERFUME

Figure 3.4: Glass perfume bottle stopper found at the Fair Play Plantation enslaved village.

Source: Felicia J. Fricke.

During the early 18th century the number and variety of religious buildings in Oranjestad increased in order to cater to Catholic, Anglican, and Jewish inhabitants (Barka 2001, 82-92). Efforts by the white elites to control the enslaved population through the Dutch Reformed Church ultimately failed, as they adopted religious traditions which spoke more to their circumstances and cultural backgrounds (Miller and Gilmore III 2016, 56-78). These traditions consisted primarily of Methodism and Obeah.

This photograph shows a small white glass perfume bottle stopper found in a storage pit at Fair Play enslaved village. The photograph does not quite capture its beauty: if you hold it up to the light it begins to sparkle. The physical properties of an object (like size, weight, colour, and texture) have an effect on its meanings, functions, and relationship with humans (Preston 2000, 22-49), as does the context (archaeological, in terms of the exact place where the object was found, as well as social, historical, religious, and economic). It is therefore necessary to consider the various possible meanings of this object in its context.

There is a chance that its presence in a storage pit is due to the engagement of enslaved people in the monetary economy (as discussed above) or that someone who lived in the enslaved village was given it as a gift (Cook and Stelten 2014). However, the wider context of African American and Afro-Caribbean ritual deposits suggests an alternative function for this glittery and isolated perfume bottle stopper. As mentioned in Chapter 2, such objects can represent a liminal space associated with the ancestors, and function as an amulet to attract positive spirits (Leone and Fry 1999, 372-403). They may therefore have a role in *Obeah* religious traditions. Obeah is a belief system widespread across the British Caribbean islands. The word probably has an Ashanti root in the words *obayifo* (wizard) and *obeye* (witch) (see Fernandez Olmos and Paravisini-Gebert 2011: 155). However, the traditions that it consists of are influenced by many different West African belief systems referring to the interaction of humans with the supernatural (Frey and Wood 2003, 384-404). It is similar to other African-influenced belief systems in the Americas such as Haitian Vodou and Jamaican Myalism (Fernandez Olmos and Paravisini-Gebert 2011: 155-171).

Like these other belief systems, Obeah is associated with bush medicine and is often practised by religious specialists (Handler 2000, 57-90). This is because episodes of illness or injury may be connected to supernatural events and beings such as spirits or curses (see Fernandez Olmos and Paravisini-Gebert 2011: 155-170). A medicine bottle fragment found at the Fair Play Plantation enslaved village may indicate that the enslaved people here also occasionally had access to European medicines. Western medical professionals were sometimes available to treat enslaved people on Caribbean plantations, although this was primarily in order to maintain the health of the workforce and may have neglected elderly, disabled, or chronically ill individuals (Reifschneider 2018). Today, Obeah is often associated with *superstition*, which is defined by the Oxford English Dictionary as:

> Religious belief or practice considered to be irrational, unfounded, or based on fear or ignorance. *(OED Online 2017)*

The word therefore has negative connotations, and this viewpoint is probably related to modern Christian beliefs since oral historical accounts also associate Obeah with the devil (EUX-OH-06) and describe it as shameful and secret (EUX-OH-10). A similar reluctance to discuss or advertise the topic has been observed by Wilkie and Farnsworth (2005: 199) in the modern Bahamas and by Handler (2000, 57-90) in 19th century Barbados. Although Obeah could indeed be used to manipulate other people, it could also have positive influences. Harm, love, and protection are the three most important functions of Obeah (Wilkie and Farnsworth 2005).

> EUX-OH-06: And even with husbands and wives, I want to fall in love with you, I try to get you through *Obeah* [...] people believe in when you come to the house if I stand in the door and I going backwards [...] they believe I'm taking out somebody in the house by death.

Methodism came to have a much more visible (and in modern times, respected) effect upon the enslaved community. Its principle of brotherhood and salvation for all was very attractive (Olwig 1990, 93-114). Meanwhile, the Dutch Reformed Church had a strong connection to the elites and preached frugality even while existing in the environment of upper-class Caribbean excess, which must have seemed ridiculous to enslaved people trying to survive on very little (Miller and Gilmore III 2016, 56-78). On nearby Nevis, landowners were at first worried that Methodism might encourage enslaved people to see themselves as equal in the eyes of God, and rebel. However, missionaries eventually managed to convince the authorities that Methodism could actually help maintain the status quo by encouraging enslaved people to accept their lot and behave according to the rules of Protestant respectability (Olwig 1990, 93-114). The role of Methodism on Nevis was therefore quite similar to the role of the Catholic Church in Curaçao (see Allen 2017, 99-112). However, towards the end of the 18th century a Methodist preacher and former enslaved man called Black Harry arrived in St Eustatius on a ship from the United States (EUX-OH-01; EUX-OH-03; EUX-OH-10). He quickly converted large numbers of enslaved people whom he would lead in inspiring sermons which could cause the congregants to enter a trance state (EUX-OH-01), and provided not only hope, support, and escapism (EUX-OH-07) but also a way for enslaved people to communicate and resist authority. It was very difficult for the masters and overseers to remove enslaved people once they had entered a trance state (EUX-OH-03). Because Methodism was confined mainly to the enslaved African and African-descendant population of St Eustatius (Gilmore III 2005: 292), it is very important to address marginalised narratives on this topic. In the words of Charles Arnold, who was interviewed by Vivian Graham and Julia Crane in the 1980s:

> During slavery they didn't allow 'em religious services at all. And there was a fellow came in here and he got the idea o' Methodism someplace, wherever he got it. And he's pretty well known in history. They called him "Black Harry". The first experience they had in the Christian faith was when Harry came here. In the Methodist churches he's well known, and there's quite a lot o' writing about him. He established the church. He established – they didn't know when they banish him from here, so nobody knew anything about him much, only he brought in Methodism. He start to preach religion to the people. And up there on Paramira where it turns when you're going to the

airport, when you come up by that first turn there, there's a big tamarind tree there that they tied him and whip him. We don't know exactly the tree, but it was told that that's where they tied him up and whip him. And the Governor then, he was very severe against the slaves meetin' religiously. And they couldn't meet. And after Harry start preachin' religion to them, well, they had him properly whipped and they shipped him off the island so nobody knew where he came from or where he went after he left here. There is no record o' that at all. *(Crane 1999: 12)*

In stark contrast to the career of Methodist missionaries on Nevis, Black Harry became a nuisance which the authorities refused to tolerate. His story ends with him being expelled from the island for causing a disturbance. Statians are sometimes reluctant to talk about him because he is said to have cursed the island in retaliation for his expulsion, and that this has caused the island's lasting poor economic circumstances (EUX-OH-01; EUX-OH-10). However, Methodism continues to thrive even without Black Harry and in 2013 still claimed 22% of the island's population (Omnibus Survey Dutch Caribbean 2014). Methodist and Obeah beliefs interacted to produce traditional life- and death-ways which can allow archaeology to give us extraordinary insights into their lives. The following section explores this interaction at work on one Statian sugar plantation.

WITTEN HOEK

Figure 3.5: Pewter spoon and iron alloy object (possibly a a bosun's whistle) found in a burial at Witten Hoek.

Source: Felicia J. Fricke.

This picture shows the remains of a pewter spoon (top) and a rusted iron implement (bottom) which may be a bosun's whistle. They were found in the grave of an older individual (sex unknown) buried at Witten Hoek, an area on the slopes of the volcano at the southern end of the island, and with a view over the cliffs towards St Kitt's. In May 2005 archaeologists from SECAR were called to a private property in this area. Three burials had been uncovered during the excavation of house foundations. They contained ceramics of a late 18th to early 19th century date, including creamware, Afro-Caribbean ware, and the base of a sugar jar (Gilmore III and Raes 2011).

Historically, this land may have been part of Jan Gordon's plantation (according to a map from 1775) or may have been situated on the border between Johnston's and Barnes' plantations (according to a map from 1781). The graves were oriented east-west with the head to the west (Gilmore III and Raes 2011), which is standard for Christian burials of the period, and also often observed in Caribbean enslaved burial grounds (Delle and Fellows 2014, 474-492). Spoons in African American burials have sometimes been interpreted as protective charms (Franklin 2004: 215). Alternatively, grave goods may be the last things that the buried person touched in life, a way of preventing the spirit from wandering (Farris Thompson 1990, 148-184).

The skeletons from Witten Hoek are incomplete and poorly preserved. However, these burials are important because they are the only human remains that have yet been excavated from a Statian plantation. Despite their condition, they allow us to explore the working lives and belief systems of these individuals. An adult (possibly a male) at this site was buried with several dog teeth, an iron nail, a magpie shell (*Cittarium pica*, a type of edible whelk), potsherds, a sherd of glass, and a flat circular iron object (Gilmore III and Raes 2011). These artefacts are reminiscent of ritual deposits in other Afro-Caribbean or African American contexts, such as a lockbox from Saba which contained human teeth, iron nails, animal remains, and shells (Laffoon, Mickleburgh, and Espersen 2018, 350-365), and the bundle found under the floor of an 18th century town house in Annapolis, Maryland, which contained nails and glass objects. Such deposits may be used to deter evil spirits and bad luck (Leone 2008).

The older individual (probably over 50 years of age at death, but osteologists cannot be more specific than this because everyone's skeleton degenerates at a different rate) buried with the spoon and whistle, despite heavy fragmentation, had several skeletal changes which help us to imagine their life. Firstly, there was new bone formation (striated, which means it was healing) bilaterally on the shin bones. This is known as *tibial periostitis* and is often linked to non-specific infections as well as to metabolic disease (Geber and Murphy 2012, 512-524; Weston 2008, 48-59). However, the shins are also very vulnerable to damage while walking, running etc. may also display periostitis in stressed individuals with weakened immune systems (Roberts and Manchester 2010: 172-174).

This individual also had a completely edentulous mandible. Widespread tooth loss can be linked to vitamin C deficiency (scurvy) (Snoddy et al. 2018, 1-20). As mentioned in Chapter 2, scurvy has an association with sailing because of fresh food shortages on board ship (Ortner 2003: 387), which is interesting in this context because of the possible bosun's whistle (Gilmore III and Raes 2011). Bosun (or boatswain) is a very specific nautical job which requires a high level of skill. Statian enslaved men were sometimes permitted to leave the island to work at sea (Gilmore III 2006a, 70-89) in a system which may have been similar to that of Curaçaoan temporary manumission (Rupert 2012: 103-104). Scurvy (causing tibial periostitis, porotic hyperostosis and tooth loss) therefore remains a possible diagnosis, but alternatives include anaemia (causing porotic hyperostosis and tibial periostitis) or non-specific infection combined with advanced gum disease (Geber and Murphy 2012, 512-524; Ogden 2008, 285-309; Weston 2008, 48-59; Ortner 2003: 387). In any case, at the time of death this individual had probably experienced numerous physiological insults and the loss of their teeth. This would have affected their appearance and ability to eat normal food. Towards the end of their life this individual may have become one of the less productive enslaved people whom Statian masters were so keen to get rid of (Gilmore III 2006a, 70-89).

Enslaved burial grounds like the one at Witten Hoek were often located close to the enslaved village, and there may indeed have been a village to the north of these burials, although this area is currently under a building (Gilmore III and Raes 2011). House-yard burials (when the person is buried in the yard area) emphasise the importance of this domestic space, linking the community to the place where they live (Delle and Fellows 2014, 474-492; Armstrong and Fleischman 2003, 33-65).

Other excavations have shown that the houses built by enslaved people on St Eustatius were often constructed with wattle and daub, or with posts and boards (Cook and Stelten 2014; Stelten 2013). The use of these resources probably indicates that the houses were principally designed and built by the enslaved people themselves. Like the kunuku house in Curaçao, they probably represent syncretic interactions between African (for example Yoruba), Indigenous Caribbean, and European house designs (Vlach 1976, 57-70).

> EUX-OH-01: ... our huts was built more or less to accommodate, you know, the weather, because also here was hot and humid, so some of them was built in the sense for ventilation and some of them was also plastered with manure and cattle dung [...] manure with a mixture with lime or trass [...] They would sleep on the naked ground or they will place skins or mats for resting, or cane trash, you know, grass.

The site plans from the enslaved villages at Schotsenhoek and Fair Play plantations also show empty open spaces around the buildings. This lack of artefact scatter across the ground surface may be due to the utilisation of the African tradition of yard-sweeping, which renders these spaces archaeologically sterile (Armstrong and Kelly 2000, 369-397). Indeed, one of Julia Crane's interviewees mentioned the importance of keeping these outdoor domestic spaces clean (Crane 1999: 362). As mentioned in

Chapter 2, yard-sweeping has a spiritual aspect as well as a practical one, being intended to keep away bad spirits. It may have been primarily the responsibility of older enslaved women (Battle-Baptiste 2010, 81-94). In general, the outdoor area represents a space in which the community came together and formed close social bonds that helped them to survive and resist (EUX-OH-02; EUX-OH-08). There were many things that bound these communities, including altruism, trade, religion, culture, and necessity. The following section will discuss an object which represents all of these things.

THE BLUE BEADS

Figure 3.6: Five-sided blue glass replica bead by Jo Bean (left) and blue glass marble bead from Ghana (right).

Source: Felicia J. Fricke.

These beads fall into a group known locally as the *Statia blue beads*, although some of them are white rather than blue and not all of them are shaped like these ones. I should confess that neither of the beads in the photograph is authentic: the one on the left is a replica made by Saban glassworker Jo Bean, while the one on the right is actually from Ghana and I bought it for ten US dollars at the Scubaqua Dive Centre in Oranjestad. The necessity for local businesses to sell replicas and beads from Ghana is proof of the huge impact that the blue beads have had on Statian ideology and economy. The prospect of finding a blue bead on the seabed attracts many divers to the island, and there are also local people who have made a hobby of collecting them. They can even be seen on the Statian coat of arms. In addition, there is a local legend that the blue bead *finds you* (EUX-OH-02) rather than the other way around.

There are two huge problems with the Statia blue beads. The divers (mostly tourists) who search so keenly for sparkling blue on the seabed are actually looters. They pick the beads out of their archaeological context (which renders them archaeologically meaningless), and they take them home, which is illegal. It is *allowed*, but it is officially illegal, and although it benefits Statian tourism in the short term it relies on a finite resource that will one day disappear. People who remember the island thirty or forty years ago recount blue beads fillings the gutters of Oranjestad after a rainstorm. These days, the gutters are empty.

The second problem with the blue beads is that archaeologists have until now studied them with a decidedly western eye. Although they have encountered oral historical testimonies on the use of the blue beads by enslaved people, they have never properly recorded them or entertained them as fact. Given the sensitive nature of the topic, our questions about the blue beads cannot be answered using archaeology alone. The interpretations put forward here therefore use historical, archaeological, and oral historical evidence, with a particular focus on the original oral historical narratives. Heritage specialists are few and far between in the Caribbean, but this does not give us the right to control heritage with its important implications for tourism, politics, and culture (Meskell 2005, 123-146). We should therefore re-examine who we consider to be an expert in the given research area.

The blue beads were manufactured from the 17th century onwards, probably in Germany or Austria, and traded by the Dutch on the west coast of Africa, after which they may have arrived in the Caribbean as ballast or with the enslaved people themselves (Karklins 2019; Karklins and Barka 1989, 55-80). Beads (especially blue ones) were worn both ornamentally and as protective or curative charms in West and Central Africa, and this echoes the importance of the colour blue as protective in Curaçao and elsewhere in the Americas (Stine, Cabak, and Groover 1996, 49-75). High percentages of blue glass beads are often found at enslaved sites, for example at Rich Neck in Virginia (Franklin 2004: 127). At the Newton Plantation enslaved burial ground in Barbados, one man was buried wearing a string of blue beads around his neck. He has been interpreted as an Obeah man (Karklins and Barka 1989, 55-80). In West Africa, they could also be worn around the waist, by men or by women, and for a variety of reasons relating to status, identity, and beauty (Chan 2007: 140-141). Indeed, they are still used as items of personal adornment in Ghana today:

> EUX-OH-10: a lot of the enslaved Africans that came to Statia were shipped from the Gold Coast, from Ghana, what is now Ghana. And lo and behold, when I was in Ghana, what do they sell on the market? Blue beads! They are still a normal item of everyday use.

The highest concentrations of beads excavated in St Eustatius come from potential hoard contexts, for example amongst the warehouses of Lower Town (see Soffers and Zahedi 2013). Although the presence of other kinds of beads in certain contexts (supported by documentary and archaeological evidence) indicates that personal adornment did occur amongst the enslaved population, no blue bead has yet been found in a Statian enslaved village. However, the enormous concentration of blue beads on St Eustatius as a whole does indicate that something special was happening here.

According to oral historical accounts, this something special falls into several categories. Firstly, there is the use of the blue beads as a kind of currency within the enslaved community.

> EUX-OH-01: when they worked, this is what they were paid with, they wasn't really paid with currency, it's the beads.

> EUX-OH-02: what can you [do] with that if you can't trade it anywhere else? […] I think it was unfair […] if they wanted to pay them then pay them in real money, but I think that was still sort of a disrespect towards them.

Although this allowed them to trade amongst themselves, it also had a negative side, as it replaced real money and therefore inhibited enslaved people from participating directly in the monetary economy. From this angle, the use of blue beads as a sort of barter currency fits in well with what we know of the psychological landscape of enslavement in St Eustatius. According to oral tradition, the larger marble beads (like the one in the photograph) were worth more than the others and were more likely to be given to male artisans and specialists (EUX-OH-01).

Secondly, the blue beads performed a function in enslaved marriage.

> EUX-OH-06: in order for me as a slave to get married to you, I have to work for as much blue beads so that they can tie around your waist. Then I can have the opportunity to get married to you. So if you are fat, I work harder.

In the American South, marriage between enslaved people might occur through gift exchange (Frey and Wood 2003, 384-404). The example of waist beads from St Eustatius also highlights one of the foremost challenges for enslaved people: that of obtaining enough food. By the logic of the marriage beads, it was more desirable to marry a plump woman than a thin one in the Statian enslaved community. With the exception of our modern western fixation on thinness, it is cross-culturally true that plumper individuals are considered more attractive, because of the link with adequate nutrition and therefore with health (Madrigal 2006: 42-44). If you cannot remember a time when western culture idealised this body type, please consult a Renaissance nude painting, for example the 16th century *Reclining Venus* by Titian.

If blue beads functioned not only as currency but also as decorations, amulets, and symbols of marriage, it may be unsurprising that they are not often found left behind in Statian enslaved villages: people would have been sure to take their blue beads with them. These detailed oral historical accounts fit well within the overall picture of cultural interaction, resource unreliability, and psychological manipulation which, we are coming to find, seem to be the hallmarks of Statian slavery..

A FISH-HOOK

Figure 3.7: Iron alloy fish-hook found in the Schotsenhoek Plantation enslaved village.

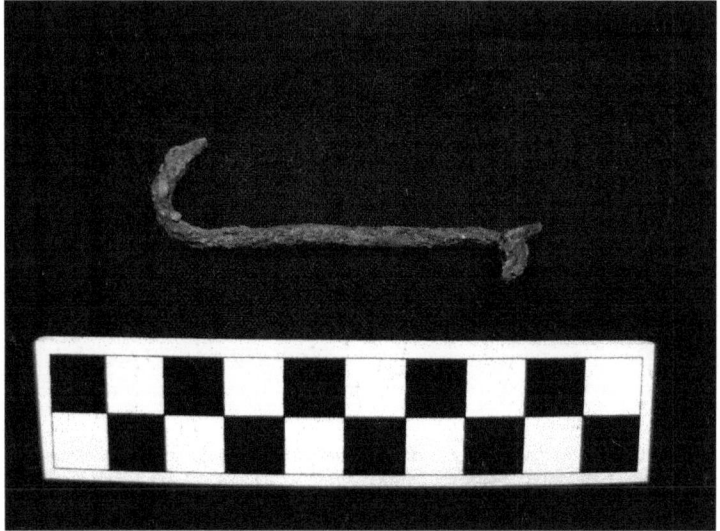

Source: Felicia J. Fricke.

This photograph shows a sturdy fish-hook found at Schotsenhoek enslaved village. The village consisted of at least seven rectangular post-in-ground huts (Stelten 2015, 291-304). They were divided from each other by five ditches, and there was a central outside hearth. Like most of the other enslaved villages on the island, it is located out of sight of the plantation house (behind a hill and downwind) affording the enslaved people a modicum of privacy (Stelten 2013). However, it should also be remembered that alternatively constructed plantation environments may be intended to serve other purposes than the separation of enslaved and free and the associated increased independence that enslaved people may therefore have gained. For example, plantations without a typical layout may in fact be structured in order to display wealth to passers-by (Chenoweth 2017).

The fish-hook indicates that enslaved people here engaged in fishing activities like those in other areas of the Caribbean. It was just one of the ways in which communities could feed themselves as well as make a small amount of money. Because previous conversations about slavery in St Eustatius have tended to focus on the favourable (albeit fluctuating) economic conditions of the island, aspects of the lifeways of enslaved people such as food scarcity and independent provisioning have been overlooked. Here, food remains recovered from the archaeological sites included magpie (*Cittarium pica*) and land crab (*Gecarcinus ruricola*) shells, indicating that enslaved people here supplemented their grown, given, or bought diet with foods that could be gathered in the wild (Stelten 2015, 291-304). This observation is supported by oral historical evidence (EUX-OH-01; EUX-OH-02; EUX-OH-08), and similarly diverse subsistence strategies were employed by enslaved people across the Americas in response to poor provisioning by plantation owners (Bowes 2011, 89-109).

Enslaved people were more likely to have eaten cheaper cuts of meat (head, spine, ribs, feet), including cracking the skull to extract the brain (Battle-Baptiste 2007, 233-248). Bones representing these parts of domestic animals (pig, cow, and sheep/goat) were indeed present at Fair Play and Schotsenhoek on St Eustatius, as well as being mentioned in oral historical accounts (EUX-OH-02). The local culinary tradition involves ground food which is cooked in one pot and then shared out individually (EUX-OH-02) (supported by archaeological evidence, see Heath 1999, 196-220), and where fish and meat were preserved in salt for storage (EUX-OH-01). The culture that accompanied these foodways was one of altruism, which encouraged the community to work together to survive by sharing food and clothing within and between families (EUX-OH-07.2; EUX-OH-05). Foodstuffs also included soldier crabs (*Coenobita clypeatus*, see EUX-OH-01; EUX-OH-02; EUX-OH-08), bush tea, johnny (or journey) cakes, dumplings, red bean soup, sweet potatoes, and yams grown in provision grounds (EUX-OH-02; EUX-OH-05; EUX-OH-07; EUX-OH-08; EUX-OH-12), making up a diet that was high in filling carbohydrates. Such diets can lead to metabolic problems such as anaemia and scurvy, for which there is evidence in the skeletons from St Eustatius. This evidence often comes in the form of porous lesions on the bones of the skull, which are formed when the bone marrow expands in response to increased need for red blood cells (Walker et al. 2009, 109-125).

There was also evidence for other types of resource shortages in the homespace. Buttons and shell beads in the assemblages from Fair Play and Schotsenhoek may have been home-made, as they are somewhat haphazardly manufactured from freely available natural materials. Similar cottage industry has been observed at Habitation Crève Coeur in Martinique, where bones were used to produce not only buttons and beads but also dice and needle cases (Wallman 2014, 45-68).

Responses to the hardships of life as an enslaved person in St Eustatius included escape and revolt. Communication channels such as drumming and religious meetings (EUX-OH-01; EUX-OH-05) were useful for organising these events. In 1848 when the French abolished slavery and the enslaved people in Dutch St Maarten attempted to declare themselves free (see Chapter 4), enslaved people in St Eustatius also rioted and demanded their freedom, and some of them were killed (EUX-OH-03 (EUX-OH-03; EUX-OH-10; EUX-OH-11) (Lampe 2001, 126-153: 143-144). During the same year, the Lieutenant Governor of the island proclaimed publicly that the people of St Eustatius were still enslaved (Roitman 2016, 375-398). The fact that he felt it was necessary to do this demonstrates the impact of the political situation in St Maarten.

Escapes often happened from the northern, Atlantic side of the island. Despite having more dangerous waves, this side of the island was less populated and therefore a more sensible choice. Escapes might happen secretly at night, or during the day while out fishing (EUX-OH-01).

> EUX-OH-06: slaves tried to escape through there, to go to St Kitts. 'Cause they get on the back [of the island], then maybe they can take a stick or a piece of wood and go across to St Kitts, it's just seven miles from point to point.

The rough sea might kill those who could not swim. For this reason, eleven enslaved people who attempted to escape to St Kitt's on the night of 27th April 1844 turned back to St Eustatius when their boat began to take on water (Roitman 2016, 375-398). Alternatively, enslaved people might try and escape to another plantation if they thought that circumstances there were preferable:

> EUX-OH-01: …if the plantation Benner's is treating their slaves good, some of the slaves will try to escape from Solomon's, who was treating them bad […] And if [Benner] says well hey, more slaves coming by me, OK I gonna try hide them, they going to work for me.

After the British abolished slavery in 1833, St Kitt's and other British islands had indeed become a good option for escape (Roitman 2016, 375-398). Enslaved people also escaped to Puerto Rico, where once baptised they could not be returned to their owners (Hartog 1976: 51-52). These examples and others demonstrate that while St Eustatius did not support a plantation economy of the kind seen on large sugar islands, enslaved people were still desperate to be free: "Now, you don't run away if you're happy." EUX-OH-10.

THE TOMB OF MR MOORE

The photograph below shows a tomb in the Old Church Cemetery in March 2016. In the distance you can see the crater of the Quill volcano, which was used by enslaved people to hide boats for escape (Espersen 2016: 154). The name comes from the Dutch word *kuil* meaning pit or hole (van Keulen 2018: 24). It is a shady, moist, tropical oasis but the sides of the volcano are too steep for agriculture and it is still an area of the island that many do not know well. Behind me as I took this photograph were the island care home and hospital, which are very close to each other, and the road leading into Oranjestad. The tomb in the centre of the photograph is said to belong to a man called Mr Moore, who died in the early 20th century. He is locally infamous and worth discussing at some length.

> EUX-OH-01: It was said he was severe for beatings [...] The way he spoke and treated the slaves was very rough.
>
> EUX-OH-10: Mr Moore was a cruel slave owner who - yeah, who had slaves whipped and punished and so forth, just because he felt like it.

Figure 3.8: The tomb of Mr Moore in Old Church Cemetery, with the Quill volcano in the background.

Source: Felicia J. Fricke.

A Ph.H., Moore is mentioned in historical documents as one of the owners of enslaved people (mentioned above) whose leaky boat thwarted their attempted escape to St Kitt's in 1844 (Roitman 2016, 375-398). The Mr Moore of Old Church Cemetery survived beyond emancipation in 1863 (EUX-OH-10), which means it is possible that they were the same person.

Punishments for running away or inciting rebellion could be severe, including death by hanging (EUX-OH-11). Lashes could be given with the *pondu* bush (*Jatropha gossypiifolia*; see EUX-OH-02), sometimes even to children. Whipping was also part of the process of enslavement when captives arrived on the island (EUX-OH-01), designed to break the person's spirit and help them to make the psychological transition from captive to enslaved person. Documentary sources confirm that as many as fifty lashes were given as punishment for certain crimes on St Eustatius (Roitman 2016, 375-398).

Interviewees mentioned the extra hardships often experienced by women in slavery, for example sexual abuse: "the master picks a woman, though she is a domestic in the house he picks her, though he have his wife he still use the slave, he use her rather." EUX-OH-03 (see also EUX-OH-01; EUX-OH-05; EUX-OH-10). Women were also beaten whilst pregnant, and interviewees were very specific about the way this was done, by digging a hole in the ground so that the woman could lie flat. This was one of the stories associated with Mr Moore (see EUX-OH-01; EUX-OH-08; EUX-OH-10). Cutting off fingers and toes and being tied to a tree on top of an ants' nest were also described by an interviewee (EUX-OH-01). In the St Eustatius Historical Foundation Museum there is a pair of shackles which give physical shape to some of these punishments. They are heavy and would have caused sores to develop on the ankles. Indeed, Olaudah Equiano described the "galling of the chains" he wore on board a slave ship (Equiano 1999 [1814]: 33). Other episodes of violence included branding (EUX-OH-01). The WIC, for example, would brand captives at West African ports such as Elmina (Johnson 1987: 31), while captives taken to Curaçao were branded at the depots on arrival (van der Dijs 2011: 116) so this may also have occurred at the Fort Amsterdam depot on St Eustatius.

Possible coping mechanisms employed on St Eustatius to help enslaved people deal with their circumstances may have included alcohol consumption, also identified as a coping mechanism in modern studies (Cooper et al. 1992, 139-152). A variety of vessels originally holding wine and jenever were found in the assemblages from Schotsenhoek and Fair Play. However, as in Curaçao it is important that we consider alternative uses for these vessels, for example as water or storage bottles (see Espersen 2019; Odewale and Hardy 2019).

Humour is also a form of release that can be used as a coping mechanism, not only by people who directly experienced slavery but also by subsequent generations (EUX-OH-08). Mr Moore, for example, is often referred to in terms of ridicule because of his tomb, which has a ball on the top. Interviewees joke that this ball is made of *funchi* (sorghum polenta) rather than stone.

> EUX-OH-10: And it has a roof shaped like a pyramid and on top of it is a ball and they would tell me yeah, that's a *funchi* - you know what *funchi* is, right? - the cornmeal, like polenta kind of stuff. That was a corn meal ball that […] was put on there because instead of it being monumental and stone, you know, to the glory of Mr Moore they made it a corn meal ball so it was not this prestigious thing, just to get back at him.

The environment of Mr Moore's life was one of decline and economic stagnation. New French taxes restricted trade and by the 1830s the warehouses in Lower Town had been abandoned (Gilmore III and Nelson 2015, 305-334). St Eustatius lost its important commercial position as trade routes shifted around the newly independent United States (Barka 2001, 82-92). After 1863, formerly enslaved people relied on subsistence agriculture to support themselves as the plantations no longer functioned, and by the 1890s most of the European or European descendant population had gone (Gilmore III 2006b, 83-96). Young people (particularly men) also left the island to find work, a trend that continues to this day (Barka 2001, 82-92). The next section will explore the lives of some of those who could not leave.

THE LAZARETTO

Figure 3.9: The ruins of the Lazaretto (leprosarium), which operated from the late 19th to the early 20th century.

Source: Felicia J. Fricke.

In 2004, Joanna Gilmore excavated and analysed the remains of six individuals (five adults and one infant) from the yard area of the Lazaretto (or leprosarium) located on the Godet property north of Fort Amsterdam. The burials were located close to the building and marked with rows of rough stones (Gilmore 2004: 35, 41, 44). They can therefore be seen as house-yard burials. All were coffined, situated in a row and aligned east-west with the heads to the west, in the Christian fashion typical of the time period (Gilmore 2004: 44). Like the burials at Witten Hoek, they represent the interaction of Christian and West African belief systems. However, it should be remembered that burial rites are performed by the living community and do not necessarily reflect the beliefs of the dead (Parker Pearson 1999: 3). At Fort Amsterdam, for example, enslaved people being held captive in the depot would probably not have had much influence on burial practices, while those living at the Lazaretto may have been subject to Catholic traditions with which they did not necessarily agree (Gilmore 2004: 45, 72). The burials at Witten Hoek described above probably reflect most accurately the choices of the enslaved population because they occurred in the context of an enslaved community on a plantation.

In 1798 and 1801, proclamations by the island government had exhorted slave owners not to abandon leprous enslaved people in the streets, but after 1863 formerly enslaved people were no longer the responsibility of their former owners (Gilmore III 2006a, 70-89; Gilmore 2004: 15-16). The Lazaretto opened in 1866, three years after the abolition of slavery (Gilmore 2004: 16). It allowed people with leprosy to be gathered in one place. This was not necessarily a kindness, but rather a way to remove them from the rest of society. Statian people were so afraid of leprosy that the Lazaretto inhabitants would have existed as social outcasts in a similar way to enslaved people. The small building quickly became overcrowded and unsanitary: by 1876 it housed 28 people (Gilmore 2004: 18). Unsurprisingly, given these circumstances, the quality of care given at the Lazaretto during the late 19th century was low (Gilmore 2004: 18).

The Lazaretto building was modelled architecturally on enslaved housing and located in an isolated position outside Oranjestad (Gilmore 2004: 17, 70-71). It accommodated lepers from St Eustatius as well as from Saba (Gilmore 2004: 16, 18). The people who lived at the Lazaretto were probably formerly enslaved people, or the children of formerly enslaved people (see Gilmore III 2006a, 70-89). Artefacts associated with the remains suggest that the burials took place before 1900, and the individuals analysed here have a minimum age-at-death of 40 years (osteological methods for age assessment often under-age older individuals), so it is probable that these individuals were born before 1863 (see Falys and Lewis 2010, 704-716; Gilmore 2004: 18). Their burials probably took place during the busiest timespan of the Lazaretto, which became much less crowded during the early 20th century (Gilmore 2004: 18).

Three of the six excavated individuals have now been reinterred. This can happen to excavated human remains for a number of reasons. Sometimes the local heritage organisations simply do not have enough room to house them: this is part of an international crisis in heritage storage space. In some countries it is required by law, although if the remains are particularly interesting, there are still ways for osteoarchaeologists to curate them for longer. Sometimes organisations can come up with creative storage solutions which satisfy the desires of both science and religion, for example by storing the human remains on consecrated ground. And sometimes the remains are deemed not interesting enough to be worth storing in the first place (Historic England 2018). This is more likely to happen with disarticulated remains (which are not recovered attached to all of the other parts of the skeleton) because there is very little that you can say about an individual if you only have, for example, one of their finger bones. Opinions on what should be done with excavated human remains vary widely, and seem to depend on the person's religious beliefs, how important they think it is that we learn about our past, and how familiar they are with the idea of osteoarchaeology as a discipline. I have found this last reason to be particularly relevant. During my years as a commercial archaeologist in England, I worked at a medieval burial site in Oxford town centre and we had an open day where members of the public could come and have a look at what we were doing. Most of the visitors were fascinated and asked lots of questions not only about the skeletons, but also about the artefacts and buildings we had found at the site. However, one woman became very alarmed when she learned from a colleague of mine that human remains excavated from archaeological sites sometimes get reburied in what is effectively a mass grave. In terms of money and time, this is really the only option. No developer would pay for each of these anonymous medieval people to have their own grave. But what really struck me was that these thoughts had clearly never crossed this woman's mind before. It reminded me how insulated from death we have become in the western world.

Notwithstanding the current state of debate on reburial in archaeology, the remaining three individuals continue to be curated at SECAR because they represent such good examples of leprous bone changes. These burials are important for our understanding of enslaved lifeways because leprosy is a disease that thrives in the conditions of poverty, overcrowding, and malnourishment experienced by enslaved individuals (Gilmore 2004: 6). They also help us to understand syncretic interactions between different belief systems, and the social isolation associated with leprous and enslaved individuals.

Leprosy is one of the few infectious diseases that have pathognomic (highly distinctive) palaeopathological lesions, which include rhinomaxillary syndrome (resorption of bone around the nose and upper teeth, accompanied by an inflammatory response causing new bone formation on the palate), diaphyseal remodelling (resorption and remodelling of the bones of the hands and feet), tarsal bars (evidence that the arch of the foot has collapsed), and new bone formation on the tibiae and fibulae (lower leg bones), especially at the interosseous border between these bones. These changes occur at the extremities because the bacterium *Mycobaterium leprae* prefers lower temperatures, and can infect nerve cells, leading to the frequent damage of numbed hands and feet. Pathognomic lesions were observed in three of the five excavated adult individuals (Gilmore 2008, 72-84). One of the other adults may have been a nun: she was buried with a crucifix and rosary beads, and it was common for institutions like the Lazaretto to have church involvement (Gilmore 2004: 44, 72). The lack of leprous changes in these two individuals does not necessarily mean that they were healthy: leprosy affects soft tissues before it affects bone (see Ortner 2003: 263-271).

One individual (an old to middle adult, probably over 40 years of a age at death) was buried with a kaolin clay pipe that may have been a personal possession (Gilmore 2004: 45). (As a side note, this individual also had a thick layer of short, dark, curly hair adhering to one of their skull fragments, and this is so rare in Caribbean archaeology that an overexcited archaeologist has written '*WITH HAIR!!!!*' on its label.) The frequent presence of pipe fragments in enslaved village contexts may indicate a kind of syncretism. Pipe smoking was common not only among European contemporary populations, but also among African ones (see Handler and Norman 2007; Ozanne 1962, 51-70; McIntosh, Gallagher, and McIntosh 1960, 171-199; Shaw 1960, 272-305). It may therefore have been one way in which the enslaved population of St Eustatius were able to continue the traditions of their homeland. House-yard burials in Jamaica have shown that individuals are likely to have been buried with artefacts that had some personal significance to them in terms of their occupation, status, or personality (Armstrong and Fleischman 2003, 33-65). Perhaps this was a pipe that this individual habitually smoked.

Evidence for other traditional leisure activities in St Eustatius have included homemade ceramic discs interpreted as game pieces or two-sided dice (see Panich et al. 2018). Indeed, the discs seem to have been deliberately manufactured to have two distinctively different faces. Documentary evidence from St Eustatius mentions enslaved people gambling, so this is one possible activity that these discs could have been used for (Gilmore III 2006a, 70-89). Alternatively, they may have been used for an African type of *mancala* or other board game (see Abdulcarimo 2001: 116-117; Samford 1996, 87-114). The assemblages also included ceramic marbles (glazed and therefore commercially produced, see Chan 2007: 178). Oral historical accounts also mention marbles, a popular game for both boys and girls (EUX-OH-05; EUX-OH-09). This assemblage therefore includes leisure items used by both adults and children in St Eustatius.

Statian music, another important leisure activity, was influenced by European and African cultures:

> EUX-OH-01: dances and music and stuff like that. There were musics that they brought here... some of them also learned to play the fiddle and other instruments, but they also made their own instrument. One thing I know for sure that they were well known for is the drumming. The drumming tradition [...] The conch shell, where they blow, the cow horn where they will blow.

Musicality is now a trait associated with the Congo people, who had (and have) a distinct identity on the island: they lived in a certain area of Oranjestad and had darker skin than other people. The term 'Congo' was seen as derogatory until recently, when an association with music helped to dismantle some of this negativity (EUX-OH-03; EUX-OH-05).

Other artefacts found associated with the pipe-smoking Lazaretto individual include iron nails indicating the presence of a coffin, as well as an iron sunburst which is likely to be a coffin fitting referring to the Day of Judgement (Gilmore 2004: 44-45). The remains of an infant less than six months old (according to dental development, see Ubelaker 1989) were also found in this grave. Possibly they were included in the grave fill due to the truncation of an earlier burial. This is not a startling find since a family certainly lived in the Lazaretto during its early years (Gilmore 2004: 18). Early 20th century improvements in hygiene thereafter decreased the prevalence of leprosy and in 1923 the St Eustatius Lazaretto was closed. Its small number of remaining residents was moved to the Zaquito leprosarium in Curaçao (Gilmore 2004: 18).

***

The evidence shows there is an alternative viewpoint on St Eustatius as a Golden Rock. Although enslaved people here certainly experienced some effects of their island's economic success (such as economic engagement, accessibility of luxury goods, and the possibility of finding employment off the plantation) these benefits were not experienced in any reliable or equal fashion. The rock was golden only for those at the top of the social hierarchy: Janet Schaw, for example, was not placed to give a view of the island which enslaved people would have recognised. Other data sources indicate that enslaved people here experienced the same cruelties and uncertainties that enslaved people experienced in other areas of the Americas.

REFERENCES

Abdulcarimo, I. 2001. "An Ethnomethodological Study of Tchadji - about a Mancala Type Board Game Played in Mozambique and Possibilites for its use in Mathematics Education." PhD Thesis. University of the Witwatersand.

Allen, R. 2017. "Contesting Respectability and Sexual Politics in Post-Emancipation Curacao." In *Archaeologies of Erasures and Silences: Recovering Othered Languages, Literatures and Cultures in the Dutch Caribbean and Beyond, Volume 1*, edited by N. Faraclas, R. Severing, C. Weijer, E. Echteld, W. Rutgers and R. Dupey, 99-112. Curacao: University of Curacao.

Armstrong, D. and M. Fleischman. 2003. "House-Yard Burials of Enslaved Labourers in Eighteenth-Century Jamaica." *International Journal of Historical Archaeology* 7 (1): 33-65.

Armstrong, D. and K. Kelly. 2000. "Settlement Patterns and the Origins of African Jamaican Society: Seville Plantation, St Ann's Bay, Jamaica." *Ethnohistory* 47 (2): 369-397.

Barka, N. 2001. "Time Lines: Changing Settlement Patterns on St Eustatius." In *Island Lives: Historical Archaeologies of the Caribbean*, edited by P. Farnsworth, 82-92. USA: University of Alabama Press.

Battle-Baptiste, W. 2007. ""In this here Place": Interpreting Enslaved Homeplaces." In *Archaeology of the Atlantic Diaspora and the African Diaspora*, edited by A. Ogundiran and T. Falola, 233-248. Indianapolis: Indiana University Press.

———. 2010. "Sweepin' Spirits: Power and Transformation on the Plantation Landscape." In *Archaeology and Preservation of Gendered Landscapes*, edited by S. Baugher and S. Spencer-Wood, 81-94. New York: Springer.

Blakely, A. 1993. *Blacks in the Dutch World: The Evolution of Racial Imagery in a Modern Society*. USA: Indiana University Press.

Bowes, J. 2011. "Provisioned, Produced, Procured: Slave Subsistence Strategies and Social Relations at Thomas Jefferson's Poplar Forest." *Journal of Ethnobiology* 31 (1): 89-109.

Chan, A. 2007. *Slavery in the Age of Reason: Archaeology at a New England Farm*. Knoxville: University of Tennessee Press.

Chenoweth, J. 2017. *Simplicity, Equality, and Slavery: An Archaeology of Quakerism in the British Virgin Islands, 1740-1780*. Gainesville: University of Florida Press.

Cook, R. 2015. *Archaeological Research and Data Recovery of Fair Play Plantation, St Eustatius, the Dutch Caribbean*. St Eustatius: St Eustatius Center for Archaeological Research (SECAR).

Cook, R. and R. Stelten. 2014. *Preliminary Investigation of the Slave Quarters at Fair Play Plantation, St Eustatius, Dutch Caribbean: A Mid-Eighteenth to Mid-Nineteenth Century Sugar Plantation*. St Eustatius: St Eustatius Centre for Archaeological Research (SECAR).

Cooper, M., M. Russell, J. Skinner, M. Frone, and P. Mudar. 1992. "Stress and Alcohol use: Moderating Effects of Gender, Coping, and Alcohol Expectancies." *Journal of Abnormal Psychology* 101 (1): 139-152.

Crane, J., ed. 1999. *Statia Silhouettes*. New York: Vantage Press.

Craton, M. 2003 [1997]. "Slavery and Slave Society in the British Caribbean." In *The Slavery Reader*, edited by G. Heuman and J. Walvin, 103-111. Abingdon: Routledge.

Delle, J. and K. Fellows. 2014. "Death and Burial at Marshall's Pen, a Jamaican Coffee Plantation, 1814-1839: Examining the End of Life at the End of Slavery." *Slavery and Abolition* 35 (3): 474-492.

Emmer, P. 2011. "Slavery and the Slave Trade of the Minor Atlantic Powers." In *The Cambridge World History of Slavery, Volume 3: AD 1420-AD 1804*, edited by D. Eltis and S. Engerman, 450-475. Cambridge: Cambridge University Press.

Equiano, O. 1999 [1814]. *The Life of Olaudah Equiano, Or Gustavus Vassa, the African*. New York: Dover Thrift Publications Inc.
Espersen, R. 2016. "'Better than we': Landscapes and Materialities of Race, Class, and Gender in Pre-Emancipation Colonial Saba, Dutch Caribbean. PhD Thesis."Universiteit Leiden.
———. 2019. "From Hell's Gate to the Promised Land: Perspectives of Poverty in Saba, Dutch Caribbean, 1780 to Mid-20th Century." *Historical Archaeology* 53 (2).
Falys, C. and M. Lewis. 2010. "Proposing a Way Forward: A Review of Standardisation in the use of Age Categories and Ageing Techniques in Osteological Analysis (2004-2009)." *International Journal of Osteoarchaeology* 21 (6): 704-716.
Farris Thompson, R. 1990. "Kongo Influences on African-American Artistic Culture." In *Africanisms in American Culture*, edited by E. Holloway, 148-184. Indianapolis: Indiana University Press.
Fernandez Olmos, M. and L. Paravisini-Gebert. 2011. *Creole Religions of the Caribbean: An Introduction from Vodou and Santeria to Obeah and Espiritismo*. 2nd ed. London: New York University Press.
Franklin, M. 2004. *An Archaeological Study of the Rich Neck Slave Quarter and Enslaved Domestic Life*. Virginia: The Colonial Williamsburg Foundation.
Frey, S. and B. Wood. 2003. "The Americas: The Survival of African Religions." In *The Slavery Reader*, edited by G. Heuman and J. Walvin, 384-404. Abingdon: Routledge.
Geber, J. and E. Murphy. 2012. "Scurvy in the Great Irish Famine: Evidence of Vitamin C Deficiency from a Mid-19th Century Skeletal Population." *American Journal of Physical Anthropology* 148: 512-524.
Gilmore III, R. 2006a. "All the Documents are Destroyed! Documenting Slavery for St Eustatius, Netherlands Antilles." In *African Re-Genesis: Confronting Social Issues in the Diaspora*, edited by J. Haviser and K. MacDonald, 70-89. New York: UCL Press.
———. 2005. "The Archaeology of New World Slave Societies: A Comparative Analysis with Particular Reference to St Eustatius, Netherlands Antilles. PhD Thesis."University College London.
———. 2010. "Blue Beads, Afro-Caribbean Wares and Tumblers and International Trade by Enslaved Africans." In *Freeports of the Caribbean: Curacao and Statia in the 18th Century: Memories of Autonomy*, edited by I. Witteveen and E. Francisco, 43-53. Willemstad, Curacao: National Archaeological Anthropological Memory Management.
———. 2006b. "Transformation and Upheaval in the West Indies: The Case of Oranjestad, St Eustatius, Netherlands Antilles." In *Cities in the World, 1500-2000*, edited by A. Green and R. Leech, 83-96. London: Maney Press.
Gilmore III, R. and L. Nelson. 2015. "Heritage Management on St Eustatius: The Dutch West Indies Headquarters Project." In *Managing our Past into the Future: Archaeological Heritage Management in the Dutch Caribbean*, edited by C. Hofman and J. Haviser, 305-334. Leiden: Sidestone Press.
Gilmore III, R. and A. Raes. 2011. *Shawn Lester Burials, White Hook Or Witten Hoek Area Excavation*. St Eustatius: St Eustatius Center for Archaeological Research (SECAR).
Gilmore III, R. and M. Roth. 2013. "Fort Oranje, St Eustatius: An Historical Archaeological and Architectural Assessment." *Fort* 41 (2): 76-91.
Gilmore, J. 2008. "Leprosy at the Lazaretto on St Eustatius, Netherlands Antilles." *International Journal of Osteoarchaeology* 18: 72-84.
———. 2004. "The Palaeopathological Changes at the Lazaretto Leper Colony on St Eustatius, Netherlands Antilles. MSc Thesis."University of London.
Handler, J. 2000. "Slave Medicine and Obeah in Barbados, Circa 1650 to 1834." *New West Indian Guide* 74 (1 & 2): 57-90.

Handler, J. and N. Norman. 2007. "From West Africa to Barbados: A Rare Pipe from a Plantation Slave Cemetery." *African Diaspora Archaeology Newsletter* September Issue.

Hartog, J. 1997. *De Forten, Verdedigingswerken En Geschutstellingen Van Sint Eustatius En Saba, Van Pieter Van Corselles Tot Abraham Heyliger 1636-1785*. Zaltbommel: Europese Bibliotheek.

———. 1976. *History of St Eustatius*. Aruba: De Wit.

Hauser, M. 2011. "Routes and Roots of Empire: Pots, Power, and Slavery in the 18th-Century British Caribbean." *American Anthropologist* 113 (3): 431-447.

Haviser, J. 2001. "Historical Archaeology in the Netherlands Antilles and Aruba." In *Island Lives: Historical Archaeologies of the Caribbean*, edited by P. Farnsworth, 60-81. USA: University of Alabama Press.

Heath, B. 1999. "Yabbas, Monkeys, Jugs and Jars: An Historical Context for African-Caribbean Pottery on St Eustatius." In *African Sites Archaeology in the Caribbean*, edited by J. Haviser, 196-220. Jamaica: Ian Randle Publishers.

Johnson, W. 1987. *For the Love of St Maarten*. New York: Carlton Press Inc.

Karklins, K. 2019. "Furnace-wound beadmaking in the Bavarian/Bohemian forests and environs, 15th-19th centuries."*The Bead Forum: Newsletter of the Society of Bead Researchers*, 74, 1–3.

Karklins, K. and N. Barka. 1989. "The Beads of St Eustatius, Netherlands Antilles." *Beads* 1: 55-80.

Kim, M. and J. Shim. 2019. "Comparison of Radiological and Clinical Outcomes After Surgical Reduction with Fixation Or Halo-Vest Immobilization for Treating Unstable Atlas Fractures." *Acta Neurochirurgica* 161 (4): 685-693.

Knappert, L. 1932. *Geschiedenis Van De Nederlandsche Bovenwindsche Eilanden in De 18de Eeuw*. 's-Gravenhage: Martinus Nijhoff.

Laffoon, J., H. Mickleburgh, and R. Espersen. 2018. "Life History of an Enslaved African: Multiple Isotope Evidence for Forced Childhood Migration from Africa to the Caribbean and Associated Dietary Change." *Antiquity* 60 (2): 350-365.

Lampe, A. 2001. "Christianity and Slavery in the Dutch Caribbean." In *Christianity in the Caribbean: Essays on Church History*, edited by A. Lampe, 126-153. Barbados: University of the West Indies.

Leone, M. 2008. "A Unique, Early Artifact of African Worship Uncovered in Annapolis." *African Diaspora Archaeology Newsletter* December Issue.

Leone, M. and G. Fry. 1999. "Conjuring in the Big House Kitchen: An Interpretation of African American Belief Systems Based on the Uses of Archaeology and Folklore Sources." *The Journal of African American Folklore* 112 (445): 372-403.

Leslie, T. 2018. "Colonialism Begets Coloniality: A Case Study of Sint Eustatius, Dutch Caribbean." In *Smash the Pillars: Decoloniality and the Imaginary of Colour in the Dutch Kingdom*, edited by M. Weiner and A. Baez, 39-54. London: Lexington Books.

Lewis, G. 1983. *Main Currents in Caribbean Thought: The Historical Evolution of Caribbean Society in its Ideological Aspects, 1492-1900*. London: The John Hopkins University Press.

MacEachern, S. 2011. "The Concept of Race in Contemporary Anthropology." In *Race and Ethnicity: The United States and the World*, edited by R. Scupin. 2nd ed., 34-57. New York: Prentice Hall.

Mays, S. and M. Brickley, N. Dodwell, and J. Sidell. 2018. *The Role of the Human Osteologist in an Archaeological Fieldworks Project*. Swindon: Historic England.

Madrigal, L. 2006. *Human Biology of Afro-Caribbean Populations*. Cambridge: Cambridge University Press.

McIntosh, S., D. Gallagher, and R. McIntosh. 1960. "Tobacco Pipes from Excavations at the Museum Site, Jenne, Mali." *Journal of African Archaeology* 1: 171-199.

Meskell, L. 2005. "Sites of Violence: Terrorism, Tourism, and Heritage in the Archaeological Present." In *Embedding Ethics*, edited by L. Meskell and P. Pels, 123-146. Oxford: Berg Publishers.

Miller, D. and R. Gilmore III. 2016. "Negotiating Tensions: The Religious Landscape of St Eustatius, 1636-1795." *Journal of Social Archaeoogy* 16 (1): 56-78.

Morsink, J. 2012. *Archaeological Assessment Godet/Fort Amsterdam Cemetery (SE600) St Eustatius, Dutch Caribbean*. St Eustatius: St Eustatius Centre for Archaeological Research (SECAR).

Odell, D. 2010. "Porcelain, Print Culture, and Mercantile Aesthetics." In *The Cultural Aesthetics of Eighteenth-Century Porcelain*, edited by A. Cavanaugh and M. Yonan, 141-158. Farnham, Surrey: Ashgate Publishing Limited.

Odewale, A. and M. Hardy 2019. "Royal Enslaved Afro-Caribbeans in Christiansted: Exploring the Archaeology of Enslavement in a Caribbean City." In *Archaeology of Domestic Landscapes of the Enslaved in the Caribbean*, edited by Delle, J. and E. Clay, 188-216. Gainesville: University of Florida Press.

OED Online. "Superstition, N." Oxford University Press, last modified June 2017, accessed 6th November, 2017, http://www.oed.com/view/Entry/194517?redirectedFrom=superstition#eid.

Ogden, A. 2008. "Advances in the Palaeopathology of Teeth and Jaws." In *Advances in Human Palaeopathology*, edited by R. Pinhasi and S. Mays, 285-309. London: John Wiley and Sons Ltd.

Olwig, K. 1990. "The Struggle for Respectability: Methodism and Afro-Caribbean Culture on 19th Century Nevis." *Nieuwe West-Indische Gids* 64 (3/4): 93-114.

Omnibus Survey Dutch Caribbean. "Over 80 Percent of Dutch Caribbean Population are Religious." Het Centraal Bureau voor de Statistiek, last modified 18th December, accessed 13th June, 2019, https://www.cbs.nl/en-gb/news/2014/51/over-80-percent-of-caribbean-netherlands-population-are-religious.

Ortner, D. 2003. *Identification of Pathological Conditions in Human Skeletal Remains*. 2nd ed. London: Academic Press.

Ozanne, P. 1962. "Notes on the Early Historic Archaeology of Accra." *Transactions of the Historical Society of Ghana* 6: 51-70.

Panich, L., E. Lederer, R. Phillip, and E. Dylla. 2018. "Heads Or Tails? Modified Ceramic Gaming Pieces from Colonial California." *International Journal of Historical Archaeology* 22: 746-770.

Parker Pearson, M. 1999. *The Archaeology of Death and Burial*. Stroud: Sutton Publishing Limited.

Preston, B. 2000. "The Functions of Things: A Philosophical Perspective on Material Culture." In *Matter, Materiality and Modern Culture*, edited by P. Graves-Brown, 22-49. London: Routledge.

Reifschneider, M. 2018. "Enslavement and Institutionalized Care: The Politics of Health in Nineteenth-Century St Croix, Danish West Indies." *World Archaeology*.

Roberts, C. and K. Manchester. 2010. *The Archaeology of Disease*. 3rd ed. Gloucester: Sutton Publishing.

Roitman, J. 2016. "Land of Hope and Dreams: Slavery and Abolition in the Dutch Leeward Islands, 1825-1965." *Slavery and Abolition* 37 (2): 375-398.

Rupert, L. 2012. *Creolization and Contraband: Curacao in the Early Modern Atlantic World*. London: University of Georgia Press.

Samford, P. 1996. "The Archaeology of African-American Slavery and Material Culture." *The William and Mary Quarterly* 53 (1): 87-114.

Schaw, J. 1921. *Journal of a Lady of Quality: Being the Narrative of a Journey from Scotland to the West Indies, North Carolina, and Portugal, in the Years 1774 to 1776*. Lisbon: Yale University Press.

Shaw, T. 1960. "Early Smoking Pipes: In Africa, Europe and America." *The Journal of the Royal Anthropological Institute of Great Britain and Ireland* 90 (2): 272-305.

Snoddy, A., H. Buckley, G. Elliott, V. Standen, B. Arriaza, and S. Halcrow. 2018. "Macroscopic Features of Scurvy in Human Skeletal Remains: A Literature Synthesis and Diagnostic Guide." *American Journal of Physical Anthropology* July: 1-20.

Soffers, P. and P. Zahedi. 2013. *Archaeological Excavations at Old Gin House: Remains of a Mid-18th to Late-18th Century Domesticate Area on a Terrace in Lower Town, St Eustatius, Dutch Caribbean*. St Eustatius: St Eustatius Centre for Archaeological Research (SECAR).

Stelten, R. 2013. *Archaeological Excavations at Schotsenhoek Plantation, St Eustatius, Dutch Caribbean: An Early to Mid Eighteenth Century Slave Settlement at a Sugar Plantation on the Caribbean's 'Historical Gem'*. St Eustatius: St Eustatius Center for Archaeological Research (SECAR).

———. 2015. "Heritage Management of an 18th-Century Slave Village at Schotsenhoek Plantation, St Eustatius." In *Managing our Past into the Future: Archaeological Heritage Management in the Dutch Caribbean*, edited by C. Hofman and J. Haviser, 291-304. Leiden: Sidestone Press.

Stine, L., M. Cabak, and M. Groover. 1996. "Blue Beads as African-American Cultural Symbols." *Historical Archaeology* 30 (3): 49-75.

Sule, E., R. Sutton, D. Jones, I. Igbo, and L. Jones. 2017. "The Past does Matter: A Nursing Perspective on Post Traumatic Slave Syndrone (PTSS)." *Journal of Racial and Ethnic Health Disparities* 4: 779-783.

Ubelaker, D. 1989. *Human Skeletal Remains: Excavation, Analysis, Interpretation*. Washington DC: Taraxacum.

van den Bor, W. 1981. *Island Adrift: The Social Organization of a Small Caribbean Community. The Case of St Eustatius*. The Hague: Smits Drukkers-Uitgevers BV.

van der Dijs, N. 2011. "The Nature of Ethnic Identity among the People of Curacao. PhD Thesis."Koninklijk Instituut voor Taal- Land- en Volkenkunde (KITLV).

van Keulen, F. 2018. "The Island without Water: The Cisterns of St Eustatius in the Colonial Era." MA, Universiteit Leiden.

Vlach, J. 1976. "The Shotgun House: An African Architectural Legacy, Part II." *Pioneer America* 8 (2): 57-70.

Walker, P., R. Bathurst, R. Richman, T. Gjerdrum, and V. Andrushko. 2009. "The Causes of Porotic Hyperostosis and Cribra Orbitalia: A Reappraisal of the Iron-Deficiency-Anemia Hypothesis." *American Journal of Physical Anthropology* 139: 109-125.

Wallman, D. 2014. "Slave Community Foodways on a French Colonial Plantation: Zooarchaeology at Habitation Creve Coeur, Marinique." In *Bitasion: Lesser Antilles Plantation Archaeology*, edited by K. Kelly and B. Berard, 45-68. Leiden: Sidestone Academic Press.

Weston, D. 2008. "Investigating the Specificity of Periosteal Reactions in Pathology Museum Specimens." *American Journal of Physical Anthropology* 137: 48-59.

Wilkie, L. and P. Farnsworth. 2005. *Sampling Many Pots: An Archaeology of Memory and Tradition at a Bahamian Plantation*. Gainesville: University Press of Florida.

CHAPTER 4

St. Maarten: A Useless Island?

Figure 4.0: Map of St Maarten/St Martin, showing sites on the South/Dutch side (Rockland Plantation, Golden Rock Plantation, and Philipsburg) and the North/French side (Mont Vernon and Marigot).

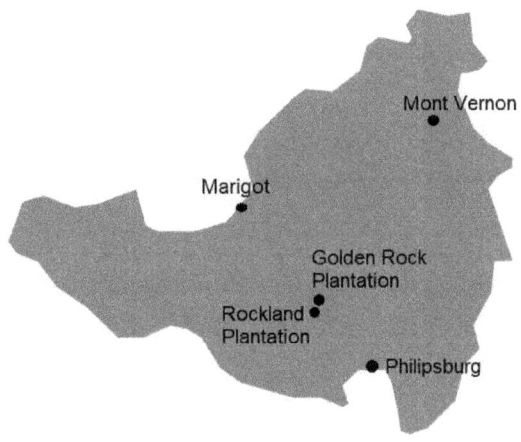

Source: Pepijn van der Linden and Felicia J Fricke.

ZOUTSTEEG

Figure 4.1: Upper jaw of a man buried at Zoutsteeg, Philipsburg, during the late 17th century.

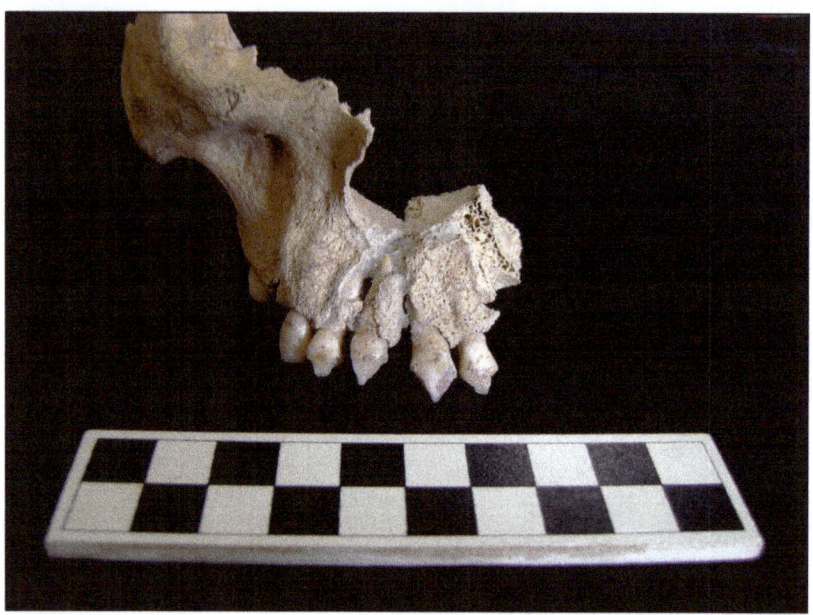

Source: Felicia J. Fricke.

These pointed teeth belong to an African man who was buried at Zoutsteeg, St Maarten, between 1660 and 1688 (according to radiocarbon dating) (Schroeder et al. 2015, 3669-3673). He was buried with another African man and a young African woman, and their remains lay undisturbed for over 300 years before construction workers discovered their resting place in 2010. *Zoutsteeg* means Salt Alley in Dutch, and it is a small southwest-northeast street which connects Back Street to Eugene Camille Richardson Street in the eastern part of Philipsburg. Today this area is commercial at one end (Back Street, which is full of shops) and functional at the other (Eugene Camille Richardson Street, which one might take in order to access the bank or the post office). Running parallel to these streets is Front Street, which is a handful of metres closer to the cruise ships and therefore bursting with jewellery shops and other tourist traps. When these three Africans were buried here, however, none of this existed yet. Instead, their bodies were lowered into a hole that had been dug into the clean white sand of a beach which separated the Great Salt Pond from the Great Bay. During this period ships from many different nations anchored in the Great Bay to collect salt, which they needed for the preservation of food, particularly Dutch herring.

It is therefore likely that these individuals were captives on one of these ships (Schroeder, Haviser, and Price 2014, 688-696).

The WIC had settled first at Simpson or Cay Bay at the western end of the island in 1631, but in 1648 the island became a *grantee-concession*, which meant that rich investors in the Netherlands could pay other people (of any nationality) to colonise the island for them. These *coloniers*, as they were called, built their houses instead at Little Bay (which is next to Great Bay on its western side) and grew tobacco, cotton, and sugar, at first by themselves but later using enslaved labourers (Hartog 1981: 49). However, the dry environment meant that the salt pans quickly became much more important than the plantations (Oostindie 2005: 13). Salt was harvested at Grand Case in the north (SXM-OH-02) and at the Great Salt Pond in the south (SXM-OH-05). Indeed, one of the Indigenous names for the island was *Soualiga*, meaning 'land of salt' (Ensing 2012: 83). These days, the Grand Case salt pond is a wildlife haven, while the Great Salt Pond is gradually being filled in for development (in fact, the centre of the pond is now a rubbish dump which frequently catches fire, sending billowing clouds of smoke over the island).

Salt picking was carried out by children as well as by adults (SXM-OH-04) and involved the same dangers encountered by enslaved salt pickers in Curaçao: damage to eyesight from sun glare; strain from carrying heavy loads; injury from wading barefoot on the sharp crystals (SXM-OH-05; SXM-OH-09); and sores on the lower legs from long submersion in the salty water (SXM-OH-01). Indeed, the Lieutenant Governor of Dutch St Maarten noted in the mid-19th century that working in the salt pans often made enslaved people sick (Paula 1993: 114). However, salt panning also allowed enslaved people from different parts of the island, and from other islands (such as Anguilla and St Kitt's), to meet and communicate with each other as well as with free people (SXM-OH-01; SXM-OH-06; SXM-OH-08; SXM-OH-09). This formed an important part of resistance to bondage.

Like St Eustatius, the island of St Maarten/St Martin had a French presence from the 1620s (Guadeloupe 2009: 20). The first fort on the island (later named Fort Amsterdam and located on a promontory between Little Bay and the Great Bay) was built by the Dutch in 1631 and remodelled by the Spanish during their occupation of the island between 1633 and 1648 (Haviser 2010c, 167-187). It was in 1648 that the Dutch and the French split the island between them, with Dutch St Maarten in the south and French St Martin in the north, although the exact location of the border was contested until the mid-18th century (Rupert 2012: 75; Haviser 2001, 60-81). Between 1801 and 1816 the English had control of the island, but after this it was returned to the Netherlands and France on a permanent basis (Hoogland, Hofman, and Gilmore III 2015, 217-231). The Dutch made little subsequent cultural impact on the island, where English had already become the *lingua franca* (Oostindie 2005: 9).

There is a local legend that the French and Dutch split the island between them like this: a Dutch man and a French man, starting at the same point on the coastline, would walk in opposite directions around the island until they met again on the opposite side, and then draw a line between the two meeting points, in order to form the border. However, the French man chose to drink wine as he walked while the Dutch man chose jenever (which is similar to gin and has a high alcohol content). This meant that the French man was able to cover a lot more ground than the Dutch man, and that is why the French side is correspondingly larger today. One wonders why neither of them decided to drink water or beer.

At Zoutsteeg, then, the bodies were arranged side-by-side, supine, and with their heads to the east (Haviser 2010b). This arrangement is compatible with Christian beliefs, although the location, date, and lack of a coffin or any grave goods suggest that they were buried hurriedly, cheaply, and probably not by the community or communities to which they belonged. They have attracted considerable international attention because of their modified teeth. The man shown in the photograph above has modifications to each of his upper incisors, which have been chipped from both sides to form points. The young woman buried here had similarly pointed incisors, but her modifications were formed by filing instead of chipping. Finally, the two upper central incisors of the other man were filed differently. Instead of a pointed shape, the inner corner of each tooth is filed flat while the outer corner is retained, creating a rectangular space in the mouth below the upper teeth (Schroeder, Haviser, and Price 2014, 688-696). There are several reasons why people modify their teeth: for example, they may play an important role in a coming of age ceremony, as they do in modern Bali (Mower 1999, 37-53), or they might be done to indicate group identity or for aesthetic reasons (Wasterlain, Neves, and Ferreira 2016).

There is a mid-15th century burial site in Lagos, Portugal, that includes African individuals with pointed modifications similar to those from Zoutsteeg (Wasterlain, Neves, and Ferreira 2016). Meanwhile, the rectangular modification is very similar to a some of those observed in both males and females buried at the Rupert's Valley burial ground on St Helena, where the so-called 'liberated Africans' who were trafficked and then 'rescued' by the British Royal Navy during the mid-19th century are buried. Their modifications may come from South Africa or the Congo region (Witkin 2011, 57-98). Unfortunately, there is little opportunity for archaeologists to learn more about African dental modifications in the Americas, partly because enslaved people did not continue the practice once they got there. Dental modifications were an easy way for people to identify runaways and were not therefore beneficial in an American environment (Goodman et al. 2009, 95-118). Other contributing factors to the disappearance of this tradition may have included isolation from the society where the modifications had meaning, and loss of the necessary expertise (Haviser, 2018).

There is also little opportunity to learn about dental modifications in Africa. There are some societies where dental modification is still practised, for example the removal of incisors in Cape Town, South Africa (Friedling and Morris 2007, 106-113), but there is no guarantee that the forms, meaning, and distribution of such modern modifications are the same as those from 300 years ago. What is needed is archaeological information, combined with modern information. But here is another problem with research in Africa and in the Caribbean: we do not yet have sufficient skeletal collections for this kind of research.

Fortunately, there are some scientific analyses which can help answer questions of provenance in archaeological skeletons. Isotopic analysis indicated that none of the three Africans buried underneath Philipsburg were local to St Maarten and that they could have spent their childhoods in West Africa, where the isotopic signatures are more similar (Schroeder, Haviser, and Price 2014, 688-696). By itself this does not necessarily provide a lot of detail about their lives, although it does assist the dental modifications in the interpretation that they were first generation enslaved people. However, another opportunity to learn about these individuals presented itself in the form of DNA analysis. DNA analysis has been difficult in the Caribbean in the past because the hot, humid environment does not lend itself to the pristine preservation of DNA strands. However, the technology and methodology for DNA analysis is improving, as well as becoming faster and cheaper. Genome-wide sequencing is now possible here. In the case of the Zouststeeg individuals, genome-wide SNPs (single nucleotide polymorphisms, referring to when one base pair in a gene sequence can vary between people and populations) were used to compare their DNA to that of modern-day populations across Africa, and therefore identify which group they are most similar to. The man with the pointed teeth shown in the photograph was most similar to populations in modern Nigeria and Ghana, as was the young woman with filed teeth. The other man with the unique modifications was most similar to the modern populations of northern Cameroon (Schroeder et al. 2015, 3669-3673). Ghana and Cameroon are around 1500km from each other: these individuals are therefore likely to have come from very different cultures, perhaps speaking mutually unintelligible languages. Rather than a group of similar individuals, we should therefore view first generation enslaved people in the Americas as isolated fragments of diverse West African societies, perhaps with vastly differing social norms. The only thing that they may have had in common was their capture and forced migration to the Americas.

During the late 17th century there were several ways for an individual to be enslaved in Africa, such as selling oneself into slavery to pay off debts, being sold into slavery as punishment for a crime, capture by an enemy in warfare, or kidnap (Thomas 1997: 369). Any of these might apply to the Zoutsteeg Africans. It is likely that by the time these individuals arrived in St Maarten they had endured months of physical and verbal abuse, alienation, psychological trauma, squalor, disease, and malnutrition both in Africa and aboard ship (Thomas 1997: 384, 414). In the event of their death, they were buried hurriedly on an empty beach, thousands of kilometres from their homeland. As many dead captives were thrown overboard at sea and lost forever, the individuals from Zoutsteeg are a rare opportunity for us to learn more about those who did not survive the transatlantic passage.

In 1690 the English ousted France and the Netherlands from St Maarten. Not finding it a particularly important island, they neglected its resources. By 1700, therefore, any trade that the Dutch (and other nationalities) had previously done through St Maarten was now going through St Eustatius instead (Hartog 1981: 51-52). In 1702 the French were able to return. The village of Marigot on the French side of the island began to develop into a larger settlement and a fort was built there (now Fort St Louis) (Hartog 1981: 51-52). In 1733 the council of Dutch St Maarten also decided to build a town on the Great Bay sandbank (Hartog 1981: 57). They named it Philipsburg after John Philips, Commander of Dutch St Maarten between 1735 and 1746 (Hartog 1981: 55). During this period the Dutch part of the island was much more economically successful than the French part (Hartog 1981: 41-42). This was largely due to the achievements of Commander Philips, who revived the salt industry; established more mills; attracted foreign settlers; and encouraged the cultivation of profitable sugar, cotton, and coffee (Hartog 1981: 56). The Governor August Descoudrelles played a similar rejuvinatory role in French St Martin between 1763 and 1785, during which period more settlers arrived and cattle ranching became successful in addition to sugar cultivation (Hartog 1981: 55, 60, 90). Despite its bureaucratic split, however, the island has usually functioned as a coherent whole. People often owned both French and Dutch plantations and transferred enslaved people between them (Paula 1993: 185). To this day, there are people who prefer not to refer to the 'French' and 'Dutch' sides of the island, because of its colonial connotations. They are more likely to talk about the north side and the south side, and the island as a whole often goes by its airport code of SXM. This is particularly important in times of crisis, for example in the aftermath of Hurricane Irma in September 2017. The hurricane struck the island directly, causing several deaths and widespread destruction. Since then, the fundraising organisation *SXM Strong* is one good example of an island-wide response to crisis that does not respect the French/Dutch border. Indeed, most of the cultural heritage of the island pays scant attention to bureaucratic boundaries. The next section will discuss a boundary of a different kind.

THE SLAVE WALLS

These slightly tumbledown drystone walls (or 'slave walls' as they are locally known, see SXM-OH-06) were constructed during the later phases of occupation at Rockland Plantation in the central valley region of St Maarten. During this time, the plantation had switched from a focus on cash crop production to a focus on cattle husbandry, and it is likely that these walls were used to contain cattle close to the industrial area of the plantation (Arend-Jan Speetjens, personal communication). This photograph was taken in 2016 and the area now looks completely different: I visited during construction work by Rainforest Adventures, who have now turned this estate into a tourist attraction with a bar, a museum, and the steepest zipline in the world. The old plantation buildings have been lovingly and tastefully restored, and Rainforest Adventures pride themselves on environmental conservation and minimal human impact. Most of the estate is now protected parkland (Rainforest Adventures 2017). However, international companies like this one have a special relationship with cruise tourism in the Caribbean. It means that they can make money from the same cruise company in many different locations, and that they have guaranteed customers whenever a ship docks.

Figure 4.2: Drystone walls ('slave walls') at Rockland Plantation during development by Rainforest Adventures.

Source: Felicia J. Fricke.

This arrangement severely disadvantages local organisations and attractions, particularly heritage charities. Cruise ship passengers are often completely unaware that the island they have briefly landed on has any locally run heritage attractions at all. In St Maarten, the money from cruise ship passengers stays within a very small radius of the cruise terminal. Tourists seldom explore the island by themselves, either because cruise employees have told them it is unsafe or because they are concerned that they may not make it back to the ship on time. They therefore tend to remain in Philipsburg, patronising businesses on the Boardwalk and Front Street, and the market, where one can buy bags and shirts and postcards of the kind available in similar markets all over the Caribbean (and in some cases, all over the world). What this means is that cruise ships tourists are neither contributing significantly to the financial wellbeing of local people (because they do not patronise many local small businesses), nor engaging in the culture of the place they are visiting. It is true that the approach of Rainforest Adventures, with their focus on environmental protection, is a step in the right direction, but there is still a way to go.

Walls of the kind that now stand within the Rainforest Adventures park were built from the late 17th century onwards and are made from stones which enslaved people picked out of the fields, making these areas easier to cultivate. They delimit properties, fields, and animal pens, and are important in helping the soil retain water, and in preventing erosion from the hills and flooding of low-lying areas by slowing the water as it makes its way downhill. They are constructed without mortar and are built up from a wide base towards a narrower top. Large stones form the sides and top of the wall (facing stones and capstones), and the middle is filled with rubble (Archives Territoriales 2015). This construction method differs from walls elsewhere in the Caribbean (including Curaçao), where there is not always a rubble fill. Both construction methods require skill and strength.

Other tasks performed by enslaved people included sugar cultivation and processing, which also took place at Rockland Plantation, as evidenced by the sugar boiling house complete with coppers (large round metal troughs used to clarify the liquid sugar and actually made of iron, not copper). After the cane was cut, it had to be crushed quickly before the juice spoiled (International Slavery Museum 2019b). An animal mill or windmill provided the power to turn heavy rollers through which the cane stalks were fed (International Slavery Museum 2019a). Enslaved people were in danger of losing hands or arms by being drawn into the cane crusher (Dunn 1987, 795-822). The juice was then transferred into the coppers, where it was heated and thickened. When it reached a syrupy consistency, it was poured off into conical moulds where sugar crystals would form while the excess syrupy molasses dripped into a pot below. One would then be left with a cone of processed sugar ready for transhipment and sale, and molasses which could then be made into rum (International Slavery Museum 2019a).

Besides sugar cultivation and processing and cattle rearing, plantation work also included growing mangoes, tobacco, indigo, cotton, and hay for export (SXM-OH-01; SXM-OH-02; SXM-OH-05; SXM-OH-07; SXM-OH-09). Domestic tasks included looking after the owners' children (SXM-OH-04; SXM-OH-07) and other chores such as cleaning (SXM-OH-08). Although domestic work may have put enslaved women in particular in danger of sexual assault, it may also have allowed enslaved people to seek approval from the slave owner and contribute to their survival (SXM-OH-07.1). Domestic workers were sometimes punished by being sent to work in the fields, as this story from the early 19th century shows:

> SXM-OH-07.2: ... originally he was working in the field but [...] the mistress took him in the house to be a company of her son. And [...] the boy, the son of the pair of the owners, went to school. And this boy, the slave boy, he went together with him. But he was not allowed to go in the classroom. So he stayed on the outside, by the door. And he heard everything what the teacher was telling. And one day the father of the house, he was talking to his son, say what did the teacher tell you today, what did you hear? And the boy didn't know what to say. And the slave boy, he remembered and he said so-and-so-and-so, but that was rude. He had not to talk that way because he was not allowed to any education. So he sent him back to the field.

The sugar heyday on St Maarten/St Martin occurred between 1775 and 1830 (Hoogland, Hofman, and Gilmore III 2015, 217-231). After this date, the effects of British campaigns against the slave trade and the introduction of sugar beet in Europe made their small-scale sugar plantations less viable. This was exacerbated by the presence of the salt pans, which drained labour from the plantations whenever a ship arrived (Hoogland, Hofman, and Gilmore III 2015, 217-231). Unlike St Eustatius, which benefitted from trade in arms and gunpowder, the American War of Independence did not benefit St Maarten because it stifled the trade in salt and sugar (Hartog 1981: 62-63). Other hardships included the hurricanes of 1819 and 1848, which destroyed the crops (Guadeloupe 2009: 27-28). After 1830, the ban on slave trading caused land owners on both sides of the island to go bankrupt (Hartog 1981: 69). The island therefore experienced much more difficult financial circumstances than either Curaçao or St Eustatius. In 1848, the French abolished slavery and many of the plantations on this side of the island were then sold off in parcels (Hartog 1981: 69-70). This was not the first time that slavery had been abolished on French land: when Napoleon was in power between 1794 and 1802 he had abolished slavery, and then reinstated it under pressure from Britain and the United States and in order to try and subdue the Haitian Revolution (Blackburn 2006, 643-674).

The early 19th century writer Marten Douwes Teenstra observed that enslaved people in St Maarten were given food and clothing, and this has been used as evidence that enslaved people on the island were better off than elsewhere. However, this is another argument based on material possessions (which do not equal a good quality of life) and on documentation written by a white man whose perspective was far from objective (Roitman 2016b, 196-223). In the same vein, some scholars have characterised British and Dutch law as harsher than French law, but in practise they were quite similar (Peabody 2011, 594-630). Many of the rules put in place for the fair treatment of enslaved people were roundly ignored. When forced to choose between the principles of repression (in terms of perpetuating the profitable institution of slavery) and protection (treating enslaved people well), both French and Dutch slave owners and legal professionals chose repression (Goveia 1991 [1960], 346-362). Areas of the French *Code Noir* that were untenable in the Caribbean environment and therefore either removed from the Code entirely or simply ignored included: the prohibition of the manumission of a master's children; the prohibition of markets on Sundays (Goveia 1991 [1960], 346-362); and the stipulation that slave owners should provide their enslaved people with enough food rather than forcing them to rely on provision grounds (DuBois 2011, 431-449). In addition, the Code Noir had always allowed that enslaved people could be tortured by the authorities and hunted if they ran away. The French government encouraged plantation slavery as a way to make the West Indies profitable, and elite interest rather than the rights of the enslaved person was their primary concern (Goveia 1991 [1960], 346-362). Enslaved people therefore had to look after themselves. The following section will discuss some of the ways that they did this.

The Water Pot

Figure 4.3: Traditional ceramic pot for keeping water cool.

Source: Felicia J. Fricke.

The picture above shows a traditional ceramic pot used to keep water cool (SXM-OH-05). The British Museum curates similar 20th century ceramic or ostrich egg water pots used by the San people of Botswana. All these material are porous and therefore allow heat energy to escape through evaporation (Spring 2009: 118), and there are ceramic parallels on other Caribbean islands, including Curaçao (Brenneker 1969-1973: 890).

These water pots were stored on high shelves inside the houses of the enslaved village. Construction of these houses in St Maarten/St Martin was much the same as in St Eustatius: they were wattle houses with lime and manure daub (see SXM-OH-05; SXM-OH-07). Their ground plan resembles other African American homes from the same period, which are thought to represent syncretic practises of homebuilding, which (as on St Eustatius and Curaçao) incorporated Indigenous Caribbean, African, and European types of construction method and ground plan (Haviser 1997, 358-375). Other construction materials included plaster, mortar, Dutch brick, coral, and iron objects such as nails (both square and round) and metal straps. What the nails potentially indicate is a construction method including the application of wooden boards to a wooden frame, also seen in St Eustatius (Stelten 2013) and Barbados (Handler and Bergman 2009, 1-36). On SXM, the wooden houses are probably of a slightly later date than the wattle houses, which were mostly constructed in the 17th century (Ensing 2012: 116).

The focus on outdoor spaces in enslaved villages, including provision grounds (SXM-OH-07.1), has a particularly interesting relationship with the law in St Maarten/St Martin, because the Code Noir actually discouraged their use (DuBois 2011, 431-449). Provision grounds have been extensively studied across the Caribbean, but little research in this area has been conducted on SXM. The only open-area excavation of an enslaved village on the island was carried out by the *Institut national de recherches archéologiques préventives* (Inrap) in 2010 at Mont Vernon in the northeast region of St Martin. Archaeologists located several domestic structures and two areas of waste disposal in the enslaved village, but did not identify potential areas where the enslaved people may have grown their food (Bonnissent 2012). More research is therefore needed on both sides of the island to ascertain whether slave owners on the French side were obeying this part of the Code Noir.

The Mont Vernon estate operated as a sugar plantation between 1786 and 1789 and between 1814 and 1850. In contrast to other French Caribbean plantations (such as La Mahaudière in Guadeloupe), Mont Vernon has a regimented layout aligned 20° off north in order to take advantage of the prevailing wind (Bonnissent 2012). However, it is similar to most other Caribbean plantations (with the exception of most of those on St Eustatius) in that the big house stands on a raised area of ground overlooking the village (Bonnissent 2012: 32, 87).

Enslaved people carried out their domestic life inside and around the two-room houses of the Mont Vernon enslaved village. Like in Curaçao, there was a tradition of cooking on three stones, later superseded by the iron coal pot (SXM-OH-05; SXM-OH-08). An oven could be made out of iron pots to bake johnny (journey) cakes (SXM-OH-05), although bread was also baked in traditional freestanding ovens (SXM-OH-02). Fish were sold 'per strap', with several fish on a string through their gills (SXM-OH-02; SXM-OH-05; SXM-OH-07; SXM-OH-08). Cassava, sweet potatoes, corn, pumpkins, and salted beef and pork were all traditional staples (SXM-OH-02; SXM-OH-05; SXM-OH-08) (Speetjens 2002: 204-209). Oral histories indicate the consumption of horse meat (SXM-OH-07), and archaeological evidence from Mont Vernon includes bone elements relating to cheaper meat cuts, for example the feet and head (Bonnissent 2012: 132).

Indeed, the material assemblages from Mont Vernon (including plates, cups, bowls, and larger vessels) are consistent with the practice of one-pot cooking afforded by the three-stone fireplace or the coal pot and then sharing out the food into individual plates or bowls (as on St Eustatius and Curaçao). Glass and stoneware fragments observed may have belonged to bottles of various different kinds, for example beer, wine, and jenever (Bonnissent, 2012). There is actually a local alcohol tradition in the form of guavaberry liquer, which is made with rum, cane sugar, and guavaberries (*Myrciaria floribunda*) (Ensing 2012: 93). During the 20th century it acquired particular importance on special occasions such as Christmas (Sypkens-Smit 1981: 61).

Domestic items used by enslaved people were often made from freely available natural resources, such as cushions made of man-beard fibres from the silk cotton tree (*Ceiba pentandra*). This was also supposed to keep jumbies away (see below) and therefore served a dual purpose (SXM-OH-07), highlighting the supernaturally charged nature of the homespace and landscape. Luxury items (such as porcelains) here did not demonstrate as much variety as those on St Eustatius or Curaçao. This may be related to the history of the island in terms of commerce: by 1700, nearby St Eustatius had already become more important than St Maarten/St Martin as a trade island (Hartog 1981: 51-52). Meanwhile, enslaved people also used the domestic space for leisure activities which were important in mental wellbeing and community cohesion. These will be discussed further below.

NICKERNUTS

Figure 4.4: Assortment of colourful nickernuts used for playing games.

Source: Felicia J. Fricke.

There were two objects recorded on St Maarten/St Martin that were used as game pieces: circular ceramic fragments deliberately chosen so that they are a different colour or pattern on each side (like the ones from St Eustatius); and nickernuts, seeds of the leguminous shrub *Guilandina bonduc* or *Guilandina major*, which are freely available in the local environment. Nickernuts do not have sides, but they do exist in a variety of colours (grey, cream, orange, brown) and could therefore be used to play games that require pieces belonging to different people, such as chequers. Other games included those which no doubt sound familiar: kites, spinning tops, and jacks (a game of catching rocks) (Ensing 2012: 68-69). It is also interesting to note that the Dutch word for 'marble' is *knikker*—tracing a connection between the activity and the nuts.

Dancing also plays a role in collective memory about leisure time for enslaved people. This is due to the recent revival of the traditional *ponum* (or *pannam*) dance by local researcher Clara Reyes (National Institute of Arts 2015). Like those of the tambú in Curaçao, the movements of this dance are African in origin (SXM-OH-02; SXM-OH-05; SXM-OH-06) and might be influenced by everyday activities such as salt panning and carrying water (SXM-OH-02; SXM-OH-06). Although our current knowledge of the ponum dance dates to the year of abolition, it is probable that dances like it existed before 1863, perhaps done primarily in secret (SXM-OH-06).

Instruments that might accompany this dancing included not only drums and flutes but also natural objects such as stones and reeds, and domestic utensils (SXM-OH-02; SXM-OH-05; SXM-OH-06; SXM-OH-07; SXM-OH-09), such as glass bottles and ceramic water pots. Late 20th century African American instruments recorded by David Evans in the United States do include water pots used in this way (Evans 1999, 379-390). One interviewee (SXM-OH-09) mentioned the use of a *marimba*, which is a type of xylophone with parallels across West Africa, although this addition probably dates to the post-abolition period (Sypkens-Smit 1981: 81).

Leisure activities also involved smoking. There are two West African-style pipes curated at the St Maarten History Museum, and many kaolin pipe fragments from the enslaved village sites at Golden Rock and Mont Vernon. This may demonstrate that it was a syncretic practice: Europeans were also accustomed to pipe smoking, so this was one tradition that enslaved people were able to continue in the Caribbean (see Handler and Norman 2007). However, it should be borne in mind that some Indigenous groups in the Americas also manufactured pipes that resemble the West African ones, so this may in fact be a syncretic tradition that spans many cultures in some areas (Waselkov 2017, 137-159).

These activities removed enslaved people temporarily from the hardships of enslaved life, but psychological coping mechanisms were also required. Enslaved people battled fear, uncertainty, isolation, dishonour, dependence (SXM-OH-01; SXM-OH-02; SXM-OH-03; SXM-OH-07), a lack of rights and legal recourse, and attitudes of contempt (SXM-OH-08; SXM-OH-09). As mentioned in Chapter 2, an internalised negative self-image is part of the process of enslavement (see Patterson 1982: 12-13). Escapist activities were therefore very important. In St Maarten/St Martin, storytelling takes a particularly important place in oral historical narratives:

> SXM-OH-03:   Stories were told under the big trees, stories were told on moonlight nights. […] storytelling was always an enjoyable and exciting occupation among the people of the island.

Some of these stories were about Bro Monkey and Bro Lion (Ensing 2012: 16), resembling those told in other areas of the Caribbean (particularly the English speaking islands), and in West Africa (Dalphinis 1985: 165). Many of the ghost stories or spiritual stories told in St Maarten/St Martin are about a man who is travelling to see a woman when something strange happens to him (SXM-OH-03). This image fits in well with the *rondzwervende man* (roaming man) described by Menno Sypkens-Smit in his 1980s report on St Maarten heritage (Sypkens-Smit 1981: 82). This may indicate that enslaved men had greater freedom of movement than enslaved women, but it should not be used as evidence that enslaved families here were truly matrifocal: diverse types of family structure may have developed due to the circumstances of slavery, for example the sale of the father to another plantation (Battle-Baptiste 2007, 233-248).

The language used for these stories also demonstrates resistance to language colonisation, for example the African double use of words for emphasis, such as *far-far* and *hot-hot* (SXM-OH-02) (Sypkens-Smit 1981: 81). Some words are also explicitly African, such as *buckra* (white person), and names like *Quacheba* (meaning a girl born on a Saturday). Creole English syntax can still be found in the Columbier (near Marigot) and French Quarter areas of the island (SXM-OH-06). Some of these words and sentence structures may be related to the African creole language Guene (once spoken in Curaçao) (Albus 2001, 443-447).

In West African countries, traditions may be curated and passed down by a special person called a *griot* (or *jali* in Mandinka, amongst other terms) (Hale 1997, 249-278). This tradition can also be observed in the *cheli* of Curaçao (Ansano 2017) and the griot of St Maarten/St Martin, who remembers the community's history (SXM-OH-06). In Senegal, these people were (and are) part of a separate, endogamous group who were in charge not only of music, dance, history, and genealogy, but who would also function as a counsellor and praise singer for nobles and kings (Panzacchi 1994, 190-210). The term is now sometimes used to refer to diverse African American artists, including rappers, musicians, and music critics (Tang 2012, 79-91). Slave owners discouraged even African names, so it is remarkable that these traditions survived (Voges 2006: 3, 36). The griot tradition can perhaps be seen as a form of cultural resistance: enslaved people continued their own traditions in a way that benefitted the community in terms of knowledge retention and social cohesion.

Griots were also the keepers of sayings, which may have included:

> A live beggar is better than a dead king.
> Mind your own business and you'll stay out of trouble.
> Meekness does not always mean weakness. *(Sypkens-Smit 1981: IV 3-IV 4)*

These sayings refer to survival strategies that enslaved people might have used, and to determination in the face of adversity. Sharing food within and between families was another way for community members to support each other (SXM-OH-01; SXM-OH-

04; SXM-OH-07). Jollification (a practice where people would come together to complete a task such as building a house) also fostered community spirit which helped enslaved people to survive (Ensing 2012: 58). Finally, religion could also be a useful coping mechanism for enslaved communities, and this is the topic of the following section.

THE ROCK CRYSTALS

Figure 4.5: Quartz crystals from the enslaved village at Golden Rock Plantation.

Source: Felicia J. Fricke.

The image above shows several quartz crystals which were uncovered by the island archaeologist, Jay Haviser, during test pitting at the Golden Rock estate in 2012. Golden Rock is adjacent to Rockland, so this test pitting was a part of the preparations for the Rainforest Adventures development mentioned above. The sequence of test pits revealed an artefact concentration in the area to the west of the Golden Rock plantation complex. Oral historical accounts had already mentioned this area as the location of an enslaved village and/or burial ground, and this therefore seemed a likely explanation for the artefact concentration. Both Golden Rock and Rockland were plantations that cultivated and processed sugar and it is unclear to which estate the village belongs. It could potentially have belonged to both (Haviser 2015, 245-270; Haviser 2012). Documentary evidence shows that in 1832 there were 51 enslaved people at Golden Rock and 24 huts in the village. Some of the enslaved people were recorded by name, including Edinburgh, Pompey, and Wilhelmina, obscure European names probably chosen by the master (Haviser 2012).

Quartz crystals like these ones form in regions of igneous bedrock. The bedrock of St Maarten/St Martin is diorite, an igneous rock, and the crystals are therefore likely to be local in origin (Haviser 2010b). As multifaceted, glittery, attractive objects they may perhaps have functioned as amulets that attracted positive spirits (Lima, de Souza, and Sene 2014, 103-136). Such amulets can be used as part of resistance and survival mechanisms because they allow people to feel that they have a measure of control in some circumstances (Chan 2007: 163). Similar crystals (artefact ID: 1000-186C-NOS—00092) have been found at the late-18th to early-19th century 'Building o' enslaved quarters at Monticello in Virginia (Hill 2003).

Such objects were part of the Obeah belief system, which has a taboo quality in modern St Maarten/St Martin (SXM-OH-06). Oral historical narratives represent it as harmful, with a particular link to curses and prophecies, for example:

> SXM-OH-09: So he did disappear like how that Obeah woman told him he will disappear and will be never found.

However, Obeah was also linked to bush medicine (SXM-OH-01), for example the use of soursop (*Annona muricate*) tea for relaxing (SXM-OH-02); communication with or reverence for the ancestors (SXM-OH-04); and storytelling (remember the focus on ghosts and spirituality mentioned above) (SXM-OH-03). Jumbies in particular are a spiritual concept very difficult to define:

> SXM-OH-06: You have different types, you got the succaneers, you have the jumbies, you have the ones—I guess ghosts is a simple way of saying it. But jumbies have never been associated with positivity. They've always been associated with negativity, you know. Spirits is one way of saying ghosts and jumbie is something else. It's still kind of ghost, but it's like – one is scary and one is spirits […] A lot of people, they see spirits, they are not – they tend to be associated with something positive. But when you say you see a jumbie, then it's like, oh, scary. Jumbie gonna get you or jumbie gonna come for you. If you say spirit you think, we think about ancestors, like something close. Jumbie is an undefined space.

Some Obeah practitioners are believed to be able to communicate with ghosts (Sypkens-Smit 1981: 49), while others can be in two places at once (Ensing 2012: 17). Red jumbie beans (*Abrus precatorius*, very poisonous red and black seeds) can be put into lamp oil to repel ghosts, who might enter the house in the evening if the windows and doors were open (Sypkens-Smit 1981: 48, 50). Sometimes these beliefs were used against enslaved people, for example as they attempted to smuggle rum over the border:

> SXM-OH-08: … the police was waiting on them hidden in the dark because it used to happen in the morning hours, hidden in the dark, but they

used to put on white sheets over their head so when they came down they used to frighten them and then come out with the sheet. They thought it was all kind of ghost, so they ran and left everything behind.

This story demonstrates the contempt with which the elites treated enslaved people. They scared them to death because they thought it was funny, and in this case it is more than a prank. Enslaved people smuggling rum in the dark night would have been scared enough of getting caught and suffering unspeakable punishments without the added fear of ghosts.

Trees also have a special role in St Maarten/St Martin stories. As the tallest on the island, silk cotton trees are important landmarks, and jumbies are said to live in them (SXM-OH-07.1). But any tree can be significant:

SXM-OH-03: the stories always talk about under a tree. [...] As they used to say, my head raised. I got a feeling when I passed under that tree.

They were used as sites for communal gatherings and punishments, and therefore became nodal points in the island landscape, a landscape saturated with the supernatural. One story tells of an enslaved person who was buried beneath one of the silk cotton trees:

SXM-OH-03: People were hung, people were killed. People were sacrificed. The tale that I heard from my parents and that is - seems to be a true tale because it our family it was told over and over. About this particular region of Friar's Bay where we see the big silk cotton trees. Silk cotton trees. They were brought here and planted in this area, they are for - when you come into Friar's Bay we have a lot of silk cotton trees which were planted as marking spots. It was marked, so if you knew that you had something buried or a treasure or gold or whatever from the ship and you come on land, it was buried and planted with a tree. That's why we have these big beautiful trees in this area. But the tale that my mother told me about the sacrificial rites of burying treasures, was that the white man had his helper. And that could be someone that is enslaved. To bury the treasure. And that person would work and dig and dig so that he can bury the treasure. But the rule was, if you bury the treasure you know where the treasure is, that's the slave, you know where it is. To protect the treasure there was a science of magic. To cut out the tongue, kill that person, cut out the tongue of that person. It was a science as not to tell. You are put here to guard and not to tell.

Oral historical testimonies mentioning Obeah also describe the physical effects of curses, for example bodily pain and rashes (SXM-OH-03; SXM-OH-09), which could have been achieved with poison. Indeed, archaeologists found the premaxillary region of a porcupine fish (*Diodon spp.*) at the Mont Vernon enslaved village. Porcupine fish are poisonous, so this find does not represent a food source. It is more likely that the fish was involved in an Obeah ritual. The neurotoxin in porcupine fish was used in ceremonies by Indigenous Caribbean people (Curet and Pestle 2010, 413-431) and in small doses it can cause numbness, headache, muscular weakness, and a burning, itching, or tingling sensation (van Gorcum et al. 2006, 391-393). The poison of the manchineel tree was also used to incapacitate slave masters in other areas of the Caribbean (Fernandez Olmos and Paravisini-Gebert 2011: 157). Poison allowed enslaved people to harm their owners with less danger of recrimination (Wood 2011, 538-560).

The material cultural assemblage from Mont Vernon also included a blue glass bead. As mentioned above, beads thought to be amulets are often found in enslaved village contexts in the Americas, and they are often blue (Stine, Cabak, and Groover 1996, 49-75). It is certainly interesting to note the appearance of this bead in an enslaved village context so close to St Eustatius, where blue beads had enormous cultural and economic significance for enslaved people. It should also be noted that during archaeological survey at Rockland Plantation in 2012, the island archaeologist recovered several blue glass beads with a white centre and an irregular pattern of facets reminiscent of the Mont Vernon bead, so this is not an isolated phenomenon (Haviser 2015, 245-270).

Recent excavation at the Frontstreet Cemetery in Philipsburg also uncovered Obeah offerings at the grave of a Dominican priest called Father Jordanus Onderwater who was a supporter of the African descendant community during the 19th century. These offerings included conch shells, dolls, cigars, coins, razors, and bottles, although some of the more recent offerings made since the 1960s may have been influenced by Haitian Vodou (Haviser 2010a, 426-441). The deposition of such objects on grave sites is a tradition also found in African American contexts in the US (Wilkie 1997, 81-106). After his body was exhumed and buried elsewhere, people continued to deposit artefacts at the empty grave site. This demonstrates the strong association between person and location in Obeah beliefs and has important implications for the archaeology of colonial-era Obeah practices in St Maarten/St Martin (Haviser 2010a, 426-441).

It would not have been difficult for these beliefs to have a syncretic interaction with contemporary Christian beliefs: in 1711 there was a witch trial on the island. One woman was thrown into the water to see whether she would float while the other had her hair cut off and boiling water poured over her feet (Hartog 1981: 53). There were also several Christian denominations at work in St Maarten. The Quakers had a particularly good reputation for how they treated their enslaved people, for example allowing them into their churches (SXM-OH-01). However, Methodism had the most impact, even allowing enslaved people to marry and be baptised (SXM-OH-07; SXM-OH-08) (Roitman 2016b, 196-223). Methodism came to the island with a man called John Hodge, a free African descendant man from Anguilla, who came to the French side and then the Dutch side in 1817 (Johnson 1987: 35). The Methodist Church came to have an effect of hope and encouragement, allowing the community to gather and

St. Maarten: A Useless Island?

communicate (SXM-OH-07.1; SXM-OH-09) (Ensing 2012: 18). By around 1850 all the enslaved people on the island were Methodists (Ensing 2012: 70). These interacting beliefs would have had an impact on how enslaved people buried each other, which will be discussed in the following section.

ROCKLAND PLANTATION

Figure 4.6: The upper front teeth of a woman buried at Rockland Plantation during the late 18th or early 19th century, showing wear to the enamel on the inside surface.

Source: Felicia J. Fricke.

In January 2017, construction workers employed by Rainforest Adventures discovered human remains at Rockland Plantation. As you walk into the park today, the first thing you see is a new wall which holds back a raised area of earth. It is from this area that the human remains were recovered, and because the retaining wall was already planned it was unnecessary to excavate the whole burial ground, or even whole burials. The result of this impartial excavation is an impartial understanding of the site. However, the information that we do have is intriguing. Artefacts found in association with the skeletal remains date the burials to the late 18th to early 19th century at the earliest. These artefacts included red and yellow Dutch brick fragments, kaolin pipe stem fragments, green glass bottle fragments, iron nails, and ceramics

(Haviser, 2017). Some of these artefacts are recognisable from other Obeah contexts, such as the grave of Father Onderwater (Haviser 2010a, 426-441).

The burial ground is adjacent to the boiling house and within sight of the plantation house, directly between the two driveways leading from the road to each of these structures. This is an unusually prominent location for a plantation burial ground. Enslaved burial grounds were more likely to be located next to the enslaved village, not immediately adjacent to the plantation house but within sight of it (Watters 1994, 56-73). Additionally, Christian burial grounds of this date are intended to be neat, with rows of regularly spaced graves side by side, each individual lying supine with their head to the west. The graves at Rockland are intercutting and contain disturbed skeletal elements, although the elements that remain in anatomical position do conform to a traditionally Christian alignment. Grave intercutting occurs when the burial ground is overcrowded or in use for a long period of time, allowing the community to forget grave locations.

There were six graves visible, containing at least nine individuals. Some of these individuals were too incomplete for meaningful osteological analysis, but the population included a child of unknown ancestry between 2 and 4 years old; two men and a woman of unknown ancestry; a European ancestry woman between 18 and 45 years old; a man of African ancestry; and a woman of African ancestry. The European woman may have been born in St Maarten, but the African man and woman were both probably born in Africa (according to isotopic analysis by Jason Laffoon, Leiden University). Most of the post-cranial remains were too disturbed or fragmentary to allow full analysis of the life histories of these individuals, but there were some interesting dental changes to be observed.

The African man had a type of dental modification similar to one in an enslaved man buried at Newton Plantation in Barbados (Handler, Corruccini, and Mutaw 1982, 297-313). The maxillary right first incisor has been filed from the lateral edges, slightly asymmetrically and with the filing angle running superior to inferior anterior-posteriorly. It is unfortunate that the other incisors are missing, but it is likely that filing in this manner caused artificially created gaps to form a semi-circle or circle with the adjacent teeth. As for his missing mandibular first incisors, these may have been intentionally removed as part of the dental modification (Wasterlain, Neves, and Ferreira 2016). The evidence that this individual was a first generation enslaved person contradicts the theory that indicating that enslaved people here were mainly creoles brought from elsewhere in the Caribbean (see Guadeloupe 2009: 27).

The African woman suffered (like many other people of this period) from very poor dental health, but in her case the dental pathologies are particularly spectacular. Not only does she have periodontal disease on the right side of the mouth at all molar positions (evidence by a *periodontal sill* formed when the alveolar bone shrinks away from the teeth, eventually leading to tooth loss), but she also had LSAMAT on all her maxillary incisors (these lesions are shown in the photograph). Additionally, there were five carious lesions (cavities) visible on the labial aspects of the incisors and the right canine of the maxillary dentition. Carious lesions and LSAMAT do correlate with each other and may therefore have a related aetiology (Turner II and Machado 1983, 125-130). Indeed, labial surface caries is found in modern populations when individuals consume large amounts of sugary drinks (Cheng et al. 2009, 395-399). It is interesting that these lesions occur in an individual who lived on a sugar plantation (and would therefore have had access to sugar cane, which can cause both LSAMAT and caries) and in a woman. In societies where women do most of the cooking and food preparation, they often also have worse dental health (due to the frequent eating one does while cooking) (Lukacs and Largaespada 2006, 540-555). This individual also exhibited contour change at the left occipital condyle and the articular facets of the first and second vertebrae, perhaps related to the custom of carrying loads on the head practised in both West Africa and the Caribbean (Stahl 2016, 38-55).

There are several different possibilities for the role of the European woman in the life of the plantation: she may have been a member of the planter's family, or she may have been a servant such as a nanny or governess. The African man and woman might have been domestic workers, as they were buried so close to the plantation house, or alternatively this burial ground might have been used by all sections of the plantation community, both enslaved and free. Uncommon in the wider Caribbean, it is possible that this is a previously unobserved St Maarten trend. Very little archaeological research has been done regarding the enslaved people of SXM, and further archaeological and historical research into the buried community would therefore be extremely beneficial for the cultural heritage of the island. The final section will now explore the life of one enslaved woman, whose story everyone knows.

ONE TETE LOKAY

The following ink drawing of a girl running with a bundle of sticks on her shoulder is based on a statue by Michael Maghiro which used to stand on the roundabout near Little Bay Pond, to the west of Philipsburg. It was damaged in Hurricane Irma and has been returned to the artist for repair, so it is not currently possible to see in public. Her name is One Tete Lokay (pronounced Won-titi-low-kay, but spellings vary wildly), a runaway enslaved girl who is a symbol of resistance in St Maarten/St Martin (The Daily Herald 2012). Her story is widely known, but even people with very detailed versions of the story are unsure whether it is true.

> SXM-OH-08: What I heard about it is that she was on a plantation in Cul-de-Sac and she was a rebellious woman, she didn't - and due to the fact she was rebelling the whole time she got whipped left and right, so she try to flee to the French side in the hills, 'cause you had a lot of, Cul-de-Sac and they have the hills around and in the hills there is a big - how you call it - cave and it seems that she used to go and hide in there, but they used to pick her up there again because it's easy to find, but it was full of Jack Spaniards [*Polistes annularis* or paper wasp] so the plantation owners were afraid to go in also. But [...] she still keep on fleeing to the French side about in the hills

and the last time they cut one of her breasts off. That is what - if it's true I don't know.

Figure 4.7: Artist's impression of the statue of One Tete Lokay which used to stand on the Little Bay roundabout, to the west of Philipsburg.

Source: Felicia J. Fricke.

Other details include her stealing food in the area of southern Cul-de-Sac (to the northwest of Philipsburg) and covering her body with lard so that she could slip out of her captor's fingers. The anthropologist Sanny Ensing notes that her name is recorded in historical documents (Ensing 2012: 20), but that does not necessarily mean that the story itself is true. The anthropologist and sociologist Francio Guadeloupe is convinced that it is fictional, and writes that it was deliberately invented by intellectuals who wanted to encourage island nationalism and anti-Dutch feeling as a step on the road to independence (Guadeloupe 2009: 14-15).

Although this particular escape may not have happened, others did (SXM-OH-01; SXM-OH-02; SXM-OH-05; SXM-OH-06; SXM-OH-07; SXM-OH-08). Documentary evidence tells us that in September 1835, seven adults (Thome, Breiser, Adee, Edward, Ellick, Robert, and Quashiba) and two children (Sammy and Jane, the children of Quashiba) escaped to Anguilla through French St Martin. Five years later, Quashiba's Anguillan partner Matthew sailed back to St Martin to rescue her sister Minny and Minny's children (Roitman 2016a, 375-398). Oral historical narratives also include enslaved people attempting to get to Anguilla, where they would be free (presumably after 1833 when the British abolished slavery), occasionally assisted by passing pirates (SXM-OH-07.1). One escaped enslaved girl may have hidden in a grave, and people thought she was a ghost. This became useful when enslaved people tried to plan a rebellion, because they could use the 'haunted' burial ground as a meeting place and somewhere to hide weapons (Johnson 1987: 34-35). Such stories played an important psychological role in the enslaved population: they gave people hope (Roitman 2016b, 196-223).

The escape part of One Tete Lokay's story is therefore not entirely inaccurate. But what of the part where she is permanently disfigured as punishment? As in Curaçao and St Eustatius, the violence perpetrated against in St Maarten/St Martin was extreme. One story in particular referred to an enslaved man being beheaded:

> SXM-OH-09: I do know about the incident here in St Maarten with a slave, a giant slave called Gudder. Gudder. A giant slave was condemned to death, to hang, in the eastern flamboyant tree on the square, the square had four flamboyant trees, now I know them personally. What I didn't know is that the one we used to play under was the gallows for Gudder, a giant slave, because he molested a white woman. The white - the book tell you that, archive told you that. This white girl fell in love with Gudder and he probably had sex with her or something and they found out and they condemn him to hang by his neck until dead in the courthouse, and his head had to be cut off and put out where the Prins Bernhard Bridge is now on a post and it had to remain there for three days, that when the other slaves pass and see it, they know, oh boy, let me steer clear of white women. Yeah. And that's why over there today they have the name Gudder Head, 'cause his head was planted there on a pole. And he was hung on the square on Frontstreet on the eastern flamboyant tree, nearest to the street.

A similar account is also mentioned by Menno Sypkens-Smit in his early 1980s preliminary report on the culture of St Maarten:

> Of course there were also ghost stories. There are places associated with long grizzly stories, like 'Gudder's Head' between Fresh- and Saltpond. The story goes that Gudder was the son of a slave woman and a plantation owner. He got an outstanding education and could play the violin very well. But he was still not declared free. He stayed a house slave with the associated privileges. When his father died, his half-brother became his owner, his half-brother who was always envious of Gudder because of those capacities which he did not have himself. He threw Gudder out of the house and made him a field slave. This could not stop Gudder from making nice music, which so irritated his boss and brother that one evening he murdered him and fixed his head on

a pole. Since then the place where it happened is called 'Gudder's Head'. *(Sypkens-Smit 1981: 47-48)*[1]

These versions propose differing explanations for Gudder's murder. However, both agree that his punishment served as a warning to the rest of the enslaved community: the display of his head in a public place, one that still bears his name today, was a violent physical assault on Gudder and a violent psychological assault on the rest of the enslaved population.

In terms of resistance and revolt, the period between 1848 (when enslaved people in French St Martin were legally emancipated) and 1863 (when enslaved people in Dutch St Maarten were legally emancipated) is a particularly important timespan in the history of the island. The French decision had wide-ranging repercussions in St Maarten society. In 1848, enslaved people from the Dutch side of the island were able to walk to freedom on the French side (SXM-OH-08), including around 90 enslaved people from Diamond Plantation near the border in the western part of the island. Unfortunately, a lack of jobs on the French side meant that many were eventually forced to return to their old plantations (Roitman 2016b, 196-223).

Methodist enslaved people were less likely to try and walk to freedom because they were persuaded not to by Governor John van Romondt, who was also a Methodist (Johnson 1987: 35). However, the situation was such that landowners on the Dutch side petitioned the government of the Netherlands to end slavery as well, wanting compensation for their lost enslaved people. The government heel refused: granting their request would have meant ending slavery in all the other Dutch territories too, and that was out of the question. The landowners could not stop their enslaved people from absconding, but they kept the paperwork and claimed their money 15 years later. Unfortunately for them, the Dutch government saw a way to save money and only compensated them half of what was paid to slave owners on other islands. They knew that Dutch owners would try to get money for enslaved people they really owned on the French side. Because the island mostly functioned as a whole, it was almost impossible to stop them doing this, and a similar thing often happened with voting (Johnson 1987: 35-36).

In 1854, the Lieutenant Governor of St Maarten, whose name was Johannes Didericus Crol, wrote that since 1848 there had been a strange relationship between

---

[1] *"Natuurlijk kwamen er zo ook spookverhalen aan de order. Er zijn plaatsen waarmee al heel lang griezelige verhalen verbonden zijn. Zoals 'Gudder's Head' tussen Fresh- en Saltpond: Het verhaal gaat dat Gudder de zoon was van een slavin en een plantageeigenaar. Hij kreeg een uitstekende opvoeding en kon prachtig op de viol spleen. Toch werd hij nooit vrij verklaard. Hij bleef huisslaaf met de nodige privileges. Toen zijn vader overleed, werd zijn halfbroer eigenaar over hem, zijn halfbroer die altijd ontzettend jaloers op Gudder was geweest vanwege diens capaciteiten welke hijzelf niet bezat. Hij goodie Gudder het huis uit en maakte hem veldslaaf. Dit kon Gudder er niet van weerhouden om nog prachtig muziek te maken hetgeen zijn baas en halfbroer zodanig irriteerde dat deze hem op een avond vermoorde en zijn hoofd on een paal vastpende. Sindsdien heet die plek waar dat gescheidde: 'Gudder's Head.'"* (Sypkens-Smit 1981: 47-48).

the enslaved people and the slave owners of the Dutch side. He said that enslaved people now worked more like free labourers, who were paid wages or a portion of the crop (Paula 1993: 111). He also noted that numbers of enslaved people bought and sold on the island had fallen drastically (but not, one might notice, entirely ceased) (Paula 1993: 112). Given their increased independence, historian AF Paula has even referred to enslaved people during this period as *vrije slaven* (free slaves). Other authors have also referred to enslaved people in St Maarten between 1848 and 1863 as '*de facto* free'. However, there was little difference in the way that the white elites saw enslaved and free people of African descent: they were equally feared, and equally abhorred. Similarities between the freed and enslaved populations came about due to the urban slavery system, which allowed some enslaved people to earn their own money; the fact that freed people made up a large percentage of the population; and finally, that freed people existed in a sort of legal limbo (Roitman 2017, 399-417). However, observations about similarities between these populations should not be used to advance the 'mildness' hypothesis: rather, they should encourage us to address more thoroughly the lasting impacts of enslavement on descendant communities.

A temporary period of so-called *de facto* freedom therefore probably had little impact on the discrimination that African descendant people in St Maarten experienced. The law certainly did not change, so it cannot be said that enslaved people gained any rights. Improvements were therefore somewhat precarious. Indeed, after the temporary shock of 1848 many of the attributes of enslavement crept back into society (Paula 1993: 116-122). It is therefore important to listen preferentially to the oral historical narrative on slavery during the mid-19th century.

> SXM-OH-07.1:   … on paper it was so but in daily life it wasn't [...] It's not that they said you know, this is it and it's from today slavery stopped and it - we don't have slaves anymore and I don't think it went like that. I think it was a gradual something.

> SXM-OH-08:   They were treated better due to the fact they were freed on the French Side and they were afraid they will flee to the French Side [...] But that doesn't mean that they were free.

A paradoxical situation where enslaved people were told they were free, and then manipulated into living the very same existence that they had always inhabited, seems likely considering the continued sale of enslaved people on the island and the lack of legal improvement in their rights (see SXM-OH-08). This situation was also likely to increase the inherent uncertainty of the enslaved person and their psychological hardship (see SXM-OH-02). For example, the threat of sale was one way in which masters would exert control over enslaved people (Chan 2007: 162).

Emancipation therefore progressed rather differently on St Maarten compared to the other Dutch islands. Some masters may have treated their enslaved people better during this period, for example by allowing the use of provision grounds, although local historian Mathias Voges (2006: 10) notes that this may have been because they now refused to provide food and clothes to people they now considered nominally free. Enslaved people were still being sold in this period, the plantations continued to function, and the census office still refused to register enslaved people (Voges 2006: 10; Paula 1993: 186).

Legal emancipation arrived, as it did in the other Dutch Caribbean territories, in 1863 (Allen 2007: 101). In the early 20th century many people left for work elsewhere in the Caribbean, for example at Shell Oil in Curaçao (St Martin Tourist Office 2016). By the early 21st century, 70-80% of the St Maarten population were first- or second-generation immigrants who arrived with the tourist boom in the 1980s (Guadeloupe 2009: 5, 11-12).

***

The Spanish initially dubbed the Windward Islands of St Eustatius, St Maarten/St Martin and Saba *islas inútiles* (useless islands) when they realised that their aridity and terrain precluded large-scale profitable sugar production (Oostindie 2005: 5). In recent years, the unique story of St Maarten/St Martin has been submerged under heritage destruction for development, mass tourism, and high levels of immigration in the late 20th century. Some people now have an understanding of the island's history that has incorporated Jamaican attributes such as Rastafarianism and King Sugar (Guadeloupe 2009: 11-14). However, it is clear from the evidence presented here that while the true story of SXM might be difficult to access, we can still conduct important research in this area. Enslaved people on the island had complex spiritual lives, they creatively resisted their enslavement, and they developed a rich culture about which it is imperative that we learn more by thoroughly investigating their homes and burial grounds using modern archaeological methods. St Maarten/St Martin is not useless in the wider narrative of Caribbean heritage: instead, it has the potential to expand our understanding of the diversity of slavery heritage and resistance.

REFERENCES

Albus, A. 2001. "For Oral to Written Literature: St Maarten, Saba, and St Eustatius." In *History of Literature in the Caribbean, Volume 2*, edited by A. James, 443-447. Philadelphia: John Benjamins Publishing Company.

Allen, R. 2007. *Di Ki Manera? A Social History of Afro-Curacaoans, 1863-1917*. Amsterdam: SWP Publishers.

Ansano, R. 2017. "What is Central to Curacao's History and National Identity? A Cultural Heritage Canon as a Tool for National Identity, Nation-Building and Nation-Branding."September 20-21, 2017.

Archives Territoriales. 2015. *Les Murets En Pierre Seche De Saint Martin: Preservons Ensemble Notre Patrimoine*. St Martin: Archives Territoriales.

Battle-Baptiste, W. 2007. ""In this here Place": Interpreting Enslaved Homeplaces." In *Archaeology of the Atlantic Diaspora and the African Diaspora*, edited by A. Ogundiran and T. Falola, 233-248. Indianapolis: Indiana University Press.

Blackburn, R. 2006. "Haiti, Slavery, and the Age of the Democratic Revolution." *The William and Mary Quarterly* 63 (4): 643-674.

Bonnissent, D. 2012. *Saint-Martin, La Plantation Mont Vernon: Une Architecture Raisonnee, Decouverte De La Sucrerie Et Du Quartier Esclaves*. Grand Sud-Ouest: Institut national de recherches archéologiques préventives (Inrap).

Brenneker, P. 1969-1973. *Sambumbu, Volumes 1-7* Verenigde Antilliaanse Drukkerijen.

Chan, A. 2007. *Slavery in the Age of Reason: Archaeology at a New England Farm*. Knoxville: University of Tennessee Press.

Cheng, R., H. Yang, M. Shao, T. Hu, and X. Shou. 2009. "Dental Erosion and Severe Tooth Decay Related to Soft Drinks: A Case Report and Literature Review." *Journal of Zhejiang University Science B* 10 (5): 395-399.

Curet, L. and W. Pestle. 2010. "Identifying High-Status Foods in the Archeological Record." *Journal of Anthropological Archaeology* 29: 413-431.

Dalphinis, M. 1985. *Caribbean and African Languages: Social History, Language, Literature and Education*. London: Karia Press.

DuBois, L. 2011. "Slavery in the French Caribbean, 1635-1804." In *The Cambridge World History of Slavery, Volume 3: AD 1420-AD 1804*, edited by D. Eltis and S. Engerman, 431-449. Cambridge: Cambridge University Press.

Dunn, R. 1987. "'Dreadful Idlers' in the Cane Fields: The Slave Labor Pattern on a Jamaican Sugar Estate, 1792-1831." *The Journal of Interdisciplinary History* 17 (4): 795-822.

Ensing, S. 2012. *Caught in Time: St Maarten's Intangible Cultural Heritage*. St Maarten: Prins Bernhard Cultuurfonds.

Evans, D. 1999. "The Reinterpretation of African Musical Instruments in the United States." In *The African Diaspora: African Origins and New World Identities*, edited by I. Okepewho, C. Boyce Davies and A. Maznui, 379-390. Indianapolis: Indiana University Press.

Fernandez Olmos, M. and L. Paravisini-Gebert. 2011. *Creole Religions of the Caribbean: An Introduction from Vodou and Santeria to Obeah and Espiritismo*. 2nd ed. London: New York University Press.

Friedling, L. and J. Morris. 2007. "Pulling Teeth for Fashion: Dental Modification in Modern Day Cape Town, South Africa." *Journal of the South African Dental Association* 62 (3): 106-113.

Goodman, A., J. Jones, J. Reid, M. Mack, M. Blakey, D. Amarasiriwardena, P. Burton, and D. Coleman. 2009. "Isotopic and Elemental Chemistry of Teeth: Implications for Places of Birth, Forced Migration Patterns, Nutritional Status, and Pollution." In *Skeletal Biology of the New York African Burial Ground, Part 1*, edited by M. Blakey and L. Rankin-Hill, 95-118. Washington D. C.: Howard University Press.

Goveia, E. 1991 [1960]. "The West Indian Slave Laws of the Eighteenth Century." In *Caribbean Slave Society and Economy: A Student Reader*, edited by H. Beckles and V. Shepherd, 346-362. London: James Currey.

Guadeloupe, F. 2009. *Chanting Down the New Jerusalem: Calypso, Christianity and Capitalism in the Caribbean*. London: University of California Press.

Hale, T. 1997. "From the Griot of Roots to the Roots of Griot: A New Look at the Origins of a Controversial African Term for Bard." *Oral Tradition* 12 (2): 249-278.

Handler, J. and S. Bergman. 2009. "Vernacular Houses and Domestic Material Culture on Barbadian Sugar Plantations, 1640-1838." *Journal of Caribbean History* 43 (1): 1-36.

Handler, J., R. Corruccini, and R. Mutaw. 1982. "Tooth Mutilation in the Caribbean: Evidence from a Slave Burial Population in Barbados." *Journal of Human Evolution* 11: 297-313.

Handler, J. and N. Norman. 2007. "From West Africa to Barbados: A Rare Pipe from a Plantation Slave Cemetery." *African Diaspora Archaeology Newsletter* September Issue.

Hartog, J. 1981. *History of Sint Maarten and Saint Martin*. Philipsburg: The Sint Maarten Jaycees.

Haviser, J. 2010a. "African-Creole Religious Artefacts Associated with a 19th Century Dutch Priest Burial on St Maarten.".

———. 2001. "Historical Archaeology in the Netherlands Antilles and Aruba." In *Island Lives: Historical Archaeologies of the Caribbean*, edited by P. Farnsworth, 60-81. USA: University of Alabama Press.

———. 2012. *Limited Archaeological Testing at the Rockland Plantation: Specific Areas of Proposed Development*. St Maarten: St Maarten Archaeological Research Centre (SIMARC).

———. 2010b. *Observation Report for the St Maarten Police Department Relating to the Emergency Recovery of Human Skeletal Remains on March 24-25, 2010, at Zoutsteeg Z/N, Philipsburg, St Maarten*. St Maarten: St Maarten Archaeological Research Centre (SIMARC).

———. 2017. *Observation Report for the St Maarten Police Department Relating to the Recovery of Human Skeletal Remains on 30 January/24-25 February/1 March, 2017, at the Rockland Plantation, Cul-De-Sac, St Maarten*. St Maarten: St Maarten Archaeological Research Centre (SIMARC).

———. 2010c. "The 'Old Netherlands Style' and Seventeenth-Century Dutch Fortifications of the Caribbean." In *First Forts: Essays on the Archaeology of Proto-Colonial Fortifications*, edited by E. Klingelhofer, 167-187. Leiden: Koninklijke Brill, N. V.

———. 1997. "Social Repercussions of Slavery as Evident in African-Curacaoan 'Kunuku' Houses." *Proceedings of the 17th Congress for Caribbean Archaeology*: 358-375.

———. 2015. "Three Early Examples of Valetta Treaty Application in the Dutch Windward Islands." In *Managing our Past into the Future: Archaeological Heritage Management in the Dutch Caribbean*, edited by C. Hofman and J. Haviser, 245-270. Leiden: Sidestone Press.

———.2018. "Legacies of Syncretism and Cognition: African and European Religious and Aesthetic Expressions in the Caribbean." Paper Presented at The 82nd Annual Meeting of the Society for American Archaeology, Washington DC.

Hill, M. "Building O." Digital Archaeological Archive of Comparative Slavery, last modified October 2003, accessed May 23rd, 2018, https://www.daacs.org/sites/building-o/#home.

Hoogland, M., C. Hofman, and R. Gilmore III. 2015. "Archaeological Assessment at Bethlehem, St Maarten." In *Managing our Past into the Future: Archaeological Heritage Management in the Dutch Caribbean*, edited by C. Hofman and J. Haviser, 217-231. Leiden: Sidestone Press.

International Slavery Museum. "The Boiling and Curing House." National Museums Liverpool, accessed June 19th, 2019a, http://www.liverpoolmuseums.org.uk/ism/slavery/archaeology/caribbean/plantations/caribbean34.aspx.

———. "Sugar Mills." National Museums Liverpool, accessed June 19th, 2019b, http://www.liverpoolmuseums.org.uk/ism/slavery/archaeology/caribbean/plantations/caribbean33.aspx.

Johnson, W. 1987. *For the Love of St Maarten*. New York: Carlton Press Inc.

Lima, T., M. de Souza, and G. Sene. 2014. "Weaving the Second Skin: Protection Against Evil among the Valongo Slaves in Nineteenth-Century Rio De Janeiro." *Journal of African Diaspora Archaeology and Heritage* 3 (2): 103-136.

Lukacs, J. and L. Largaespada. 2006. "Explaining Sex Differences in Dental Caries Prevalence: Saliva, Hormones, and "life-history" Etiologies." *Human Biology* 18: 540-555.

Mower, J. 1999. "Deliberate Ante-Mortem Dental Modifications and its Implications in Archaeology, Ethnography and Anthropology." *Papers from the Institute of Archaeology* 10: 37-53.

National Institute of Arts. "Clara Reyes.", accessed December 18th, 2017, http://www.nationalinstituteofarts.com/clara-reyes.

Oostindie, G. 2005. *Paradise Overseas: The Dutch Caribbean: Colonialism and its Transatlantics Legacies*. Oxford: Macmillan Caribbean.

Panzacchi, C. 1994. "The Livelihoods of Traditional Griots in Modern Senegal." *Africa* 64 (2): 190-210.

Patterson, O. 1982. *Slavery and Social Death: A Comparative Study*. London: Harvard University Press.

Paula, A. 1993. *'Vrije' Slaven: Een Sociaal-Historische Studie Over De Dualistische Slaven-Emancipatie Op Nederlands Sint Maarten 1816-1863*. Zutphen: De Walburg Pers.

Peabody, S. 2011. "Slavery, Freedom, and the Law in the Atlantic World, 1420-1807." In *The Cambridge World History of Slavery, Volume 3: AD 1420-AD 1804*, edited by D. Eltis and S. Engerman, 594-630. Cambridge: Cambridge University Press.

Rainforest Adventures. "Welcome to Rockland Estate, St Maarten." Rainforest Adventures, accessed 19th June, 2019, https://www.rainforestadventure.com/pages/stmaarten.

Roitman, J. 2017. ""A Mass of Mestiezen, Castiezen, and Mulatten": Contending with Color in the Netherlands Antilles, 1750-1850." *Atlantic Studies* 14 (3): 399-417.

———. 2016a. "Land of Hope and Dreams: Slavery and Abolition in the Dutch Leeward Islands, 1825-1965." *Slavery and Abolition* 37 (2): 375-398.

———. 2016b. "The Price You Pay: Choosing Family, Friends, and Familiarity Over Freedom in the Leeward Islands, 1835-1863." *Journal of Global Slavery* 1: 196-223.

Rupert, L. 2012. *Creolization and Contraband: Curacao in the Early Modern Atlantic World*. London: University of Georgia Press.

Schroeder, H., M. Avila-Arcos, A. Malaspinas, G. Poznik, M. Sandoval-Velasco, M. Carpenter, J. Moreno-Mayar, et al. 2015. "Genome-Wide Ancestry of 17th-Century Enslaved Africans from the Caribbean." *Proceedings of the National Academy of Sciences* 112 (12): 3669-3673.

Schroeder, H., J. Haviser, and T. Price. 2014. "The Zoutsteeg Three: Three New Cases of African Types of Dental Modification from Saint Martin, Dutch Caribbean." *International Journal of Osteoarchaeology* 24: 688-696.

Speetjens, J. 2002. *St Martin Yesterday Today*. Italy: Rotolito.

Spring, C. 2009. *African Art Close Up*. London: The British Museum.

St Martin Tourist Office. "Yesterday." St Martin Tourist Office, accessed October/26th, 2016, http://www.stmartinisland.org/destination-st-martin/st-martin-history.html.

Stahl, A. 2016. "Historical Process and the Impact of the Atlantic Trade on Banda, Ghana, C. 1800-1920." In *West Africa during the Atlantic Slave Trade: Archaeological Perspectives*, edited by C. DeCorse. 2nd ed., 38-55. Oxford: Bloomsbury.

Stelten, R. 2013. *Archaeological Excavations at Schotsenhoek Plantation, St Eustatius, Dutch Caribbean: An Early to Mid Eighteenth Century Slave Settlement at a Sugar Plantation on the Caribbean's 'Historical Gem'*. St Eustatius: St Eustatius Center for Archaeological Research (SECAR).

Stine, L., M. Cabak, and M. Groover. 1996. "Blue Beads as African-American Cultural Symbols." *Historical Archaeology* 30 (3): 49-75.

Sypkens-Smit, M. 1981. *Rapport Ter Voorlopige Afsluiting Van Het Cultureel Antropologisch Onderzoek on Sint Maarten (NA)*. Leiden: Koninklijk Instituut Taal- Land- en Volkenkunde (KITLV).

Tang, P. 2012. "The Rapper as Modern Griot: Reclaiming Ancient Traditions." In *Hip Hop Africa: New African Music in a Globalizing World*, edited by E. Charry, 79-91. Indianapolis: Indiana University Press.

The Daily Herald. "The Legend of One-TeteLohkay." The Daily Herald, last modified 3rd July, accessed June 20th, 2019, http://www.thedailyherald.info/index.php?option=com_content&id=29303:the-legend-of-one-tetelohkay&Itemid=37.

Thomas, H. 1997. *The Slave Trade: The History of the Atlantic Slave Trade 1440-1870*. London: Orion Books Ltd.

Turner II, C. and C. Machado. 1983. "A New Dental Wear Pattern and Evidence for High Carbohydrate Consumption in a Brazilian Archaic Skeletal Population." *American Journal of Physical Anthropology* 61: 125-130.

van Gorcum, T., M. Janse, M. Leenders, I. de Vries, and J. Meulenbelt. 2006. "Intoxication Following Minor Stab Wounds from the Spines of a Porcupine Fish." *Clinical Toxicology* 44 (4): 391-393.

Voges, M. 2006. *Cul-De-Sac People: A St Martin Family Series*. St Martin: House of Nehesi Publishers.

Waselkov, G. 2017. "Smoking Pipes as Signifiers of French Creole Identity." In *Tu Sais, Mon Vieux Jean Pierre: Essays on the Archaeology and History of New France and Canadian Culture in Honour of Jean-Pierre Chrestien. Mercury Series Archaeology Paper 178*, edited by J. Willis, 137-159. Ottawa: Canadian Museum of History and University of Ottawa Press.

Wasterlain, S., M. Neves, and M. Ferreira. 2016. "Dental Modifications in a Skeletal Sample of Enslaved Africans found at Lagos (Portugal)." *International Journal of Osteoarchaeology* 26 (4): 621-632.

Watters, D. 1994. "Mortuary Patterns at the Harney Site Slave Cemetery, Montserrat, in Caribbean Perspective." *Historical Archaeology* 28 (3): 56-73.

Wilkie, L. 1997. "Secret and Sacred: Contextualizing the Artifacts of African-American Magic and Religion." *Historical Archaeology* 31 (4): 81-106.

Witkin, A. 2011. "The Human Skeletal Remains." In *Infernal Traffic: Excavation of a Liberated African Graveyard in Rupert's Valley, St Helena. CBA Research Report 169*, edited by A. Pearson, B. Jeffs, A. Witkin and H. MacQuarrie, 57-98. York: Council for British Archaeology.

Wood, B. 2011. "Black Women in the Early Americas." In *The Cambridge World History of Slavery, Volume 3: AD 1420-AD 1804*, edited by D. Eltis and S. Engerman, 538-560. Cambridge: Cambridge University Press.

CHAPTER 5

Conclusions

THE LIFEWAYS OF ENSLAVED PEOPLE IN THE DUTCH CARIBBEAN

In Chapter 1, I explained how scholars have inadequately considered the effect that their own privileged identities have on the interpretations that they make, and thereby have failed to take into account all the many different voices required to arrive at nuanced narratives; and how studies of slavery have often neglected to address the psychological aspects of enslavement, instead choosing to focus on economic and administrative aspects which do not encompass the entire experience of enslavement. I wanted to get closer to the personal stories of enslaved people, by using a theoretical approach which allows for diverse voices to be heard whilst continually examining my own identities as a researcher. I hope that I have demonstrated the efficacy of this approach. The stories here are personal, sometimes taking place in the very body of an enslaved person; they include the testimonies of local people; and they critically assess the dominant narrative and try to examine evidence from different angles. I think they bring us closer to the past.

It is clear from the extreme physical violence and psychological warfare perpetrated against enslaved people in the Dutch Caribbean that we should abandon narratives that label slavery here as 'mild' based on economic and material evidence, or on comparisons of plantation size and type of work. These things do change certain qualities of enslavement, but the aspects of this institution which make it unbearable remain the same across borders and time periods. Material wealth does not necessarily translate into increased quality of life. Indeed, differences in enslaved lifeways observed between Curaçao, St Eustatius, and St Maarten/St Martin are mainly due to their individual geographical, economic, and cultural circumstances, and to the ways in which enslaved people creatively adapted to and resisted these circumstances with the resources available, often reflecting a vibrant interaction of beliefs and traditions that is still in evidence today.

On each island, this book has provided a perspective lacking currently lacking elsewhere in the academic literature. In St Maarten/St Martin the evidence adds significantly to understandings taken from historical documentation, including evidence for highly complex cultural and communal lifeways and a strong spiritual link to the island landscape. It is no longer possible to submerge this island under a Jamaican sugar narrative or omit it from the wider narrative on Caribbean slavery.

In St Eustatius the dominant narrative of material wealth has been re-examined. The enslaved population here experienced diseases of poverty; economic uncertainty; and psychological hardships comparable to those experienced by enslaved people in other contexts. They also developed syncretic belief systems and modes of resistance.

Finally, in Curaçao the evidence provides an alternative viewpoint of the post-abolition period, which saw social structures of enslavement persisting almost intact well into the 20th century, and human remains analysis demonstrated the processes of enslavement in real bodies.

ENSLAVEMENT RETHOUGHT

Despite such local differences between the islands, the findings of this study also feed into wider postcolonial heritage narratives on slavery being developed for other areas of the Caribbean and the wider Americas. These studies have made moves towards interdisciplinarity (often using data from several different sources, including material culture and documentary evidence) and have focussed upon decolonisation practices, which is vital in a field that is still predominantly white and operating within the colonial structures of academia (Schneider and Hayes 2020; White and Draycott 2020). Good examples of such studies have been the New York African Burial Ground Project, which pioneered this approach in the 1980s; the work of Whitney Battle Baptiste, who literally wrote the book on *Black Feminist Archaeology*; and Maria Franklin's archaeological excavation of the enslaved quarters at Rich Neck in Virginia (Battle-Baptiste 2011; Blakey and Rankin-Hill 2009; Franklin 2004). In the Caribbean, the application of such approaches seems to progress rather more slowly. Although there is an increasing interest in issues of inequality, marked for example by the recent publication of texts such as *Archaeology of Domestic Landscapes of the Enslaved in the Caribbean* (Delle and Clay 2019) and influenced by similar trends in the United States, I have found it difficult to identify many projects making a sincere commitment to address these issues. Even large, well-funded, and high-profile projects often fail to apply a truly decolonising approach. Fortunately, the tide is turning. New generations of archaeologists are unwilling to accept tokenism; they engage enthusiastically with the postcolonial and decolonial literature; and they learn from other areas of the discipline where decolonial approaches already have a stronger hold. They are also learning from interdisciplinary perspectives to incorporate sociological, anthropological, oral historical, and documentary data into their projects, thereby resisting the compartmentalisation of their universities. New generations of archaeologists are also more likely to be Caribbean people - the study of enslavement here will therefore become better able to strike a balance between the emic and the etic. Finally, I believe that the future of this subject also lies in the use of qualitative data. Large-scale quantitative studies of slavery in the Caribbean have already been carried out (see for example Eltis and Richardson 2010); it is now time to turn our attention to the true nature of slavery and the impact it has had on our societies.

SOCIAL AND POLITICAL IMPACT

EUX-OH-03 But you raped us. When the islands were producing you came and you got the salt, the everything, but now - eh? Now we are useless [...] we are still your slaves.

Over the last decade, the Dutch Caribbean islands have suffered a series of misfortunes intricately linked with their colonial history. Since 2010, Bonaire, St Eustatius, and Saba have in particular accused the Dutch government of 're-colonisation' as it takes an increased interest in their organisation (Oostindie 2013). Stakeholders see this as an extension of slavery, a further oppression (EUX-OH-05), and the Foundation *Nos Kier Boneiru Bek* (We Want Bonaire Back) has been campaigning for the re-inscription of Bonaire onto the United Nations Non-Self-Governing Territories List. Chapter XI of the Charter of the United Nations defines these territories as those "whose people have not yet attained a full measure of self-government". Currently, the list already includes several other Caribbean islands still administered by colonisers, such as Anguilla (UK), Bermuda (UK), and the US Virgin Islands (USA).

In September 2017 Hurricanes Irma and Maria had a devastating impact on St Maarten/St Martin in particular (Meade 2018). Subsequently, the Orange Movement has called for a closer relationship with the Kingdom of the Netherlands in order to better safeguard St Maarten's inhabitants from future such natural disasters (Haar 2017). Meanwhile, an inadequate Dutch response to the devastating economic effects of the Venezuelan crisis and the coronavirus pandemic have led to protests in Curaçao somewhat reminiscent of the *trinta di mei* protests in 1969 (Broere 2020).

All this takes place in a context of ongoing institutional and structural racism and the lingering psychological effects of enslavement (CUR-OH-08; Marcha, Verweel and Werkman 2012; Battle-Baptiste 2011: 45-46). However, Afro-Dutch people are resisting these circumstances and are taking pride in their heritage of creativity and resistance. There are several annual commemoration events including the *Ruta Tula* following in the footsteps of the 1795 rebels (Curaçao, 17th August) (CUR-OH-02; Smeulders 2012: 98-99), the ponum dance at Diamond Plantation (St Maarten, 30th June) (SXM-OH-06), and the Keti Koti (Broken Chains) celebrations (Suriname and the Netherlands, 1st July) (Cain 2015). Recently there has been an increasing public interest in these topics due to the Black Lives Matter protests taking place across the Netherlands in the wake of George Floyd's murder by police officers in the United States (Vissers 2020).

Collective memory and cultural trauma, which are explored during commemoration events and protests such as these, are very important in the development of collective identities (Eyerman 2001: 1-10). It has long been difficult to identify a single unifying identity for Dutch Caribbean people because of the islands' diversity, and this point has only become more salient since 2010 (Ansano 2017; Oostindie 2005: 167-174). It is now not only important to examine these plural

Caribbean identities in light of successive waves of migration in the post-abolition period (for example from China and Portugal), but also in terms of the islands' new political structure in a globalising world (Allen 2015; Ansano 2006; Haviser 2001). How do Dutch Caribbean people see themselves? Many are keen to examine the past in order to move forward into the future (CUR-OH-02; EUX-OH-06; see also van der Ven 2011: 142-143). This is an area where the current research can contribute an important perspective: one that explains, in an interdisciplinary, qualitative, and decolonial fashion, the mechanisms and legacies of Dutch Caribbean slavery.

Lastly, we should not forget that slavery is by no means a phenomenon confined to the past. Some estimates for the total number of enslaved people today reach 27 million. The figures depend on how one defines slavery - whether one includes child labourers, indentured labourers, and India's 'untouchables', for example (Patterson 2012, 322-359) - but there may be more enslaved individuals alive now than were ever taken from Africa during the transatlantic trade, and the networks of trafficking used today have direct links with those in the past (Bales 2004: 9).

Slavery in archaeology therefore has profound relevance for living populations. It is part of our responsibility as archaeologists to help amplify the voices of exploited people. Our material and intangible understandings of slavery in the past can help us to understand the mechanisms of slavery and discrimination in the present. Not only does this mean that we need specialists to conduct more research, it also means that all of us need to take more action. I would encourage readers to support organisations which actively combat modern slavery and discrimination. You may not think that slavery or racism is a problem in your neighbourhood, but these things perpetuate themselves in ways that sometimes make them difficult to detect or eradicate. Do what you can. However much the story of slavery in the past disturbs you, slavery and its legacy in the present should disturb you more.

FINAL WORDS

Almost without exception, the oral history interviewees in this study provided information on the effects of slavery that they see around them on a day-to-day basis. We experience the past not only tangibly (in the buildings and artefacts that people leave behind them) but also intangibly, in the collective memory of stakeholder communities and in structures of oppression that are still being dismantled. The concept of mental slavery is present on each of these three Dutch Caribbean islands, and has begun to be explored by sociologists and anthropologists (see Leslie 2018, 39-54; Marcha, Verweel, and Werkman 2012). Community groups are becoming active in heritage events which can work against inherited trauma. There is also a sense of anger, and a call for the Dutch government to apologise for its involvement in slavery (Nimako and Willemsen 2011: 149-183) and to incorporate antiracism, slavery, and colonialism into the national curriculum (Petitie24 2020). Dutch Caribbean people have good reason to distrust Dutch politicians, who must work on gaining their trust in order to make real change (Allen 2017). Although reconciliation

Conclusions

and socio-political transformation will require work on both sides, the majority of the responsibility for this must be borne by the oppressor.

Further work should therefore include concerted efforts on the part of sociologists, anthropologists, historians, and archaeologists, to fully explore the Dutch Caribbean past and its links to the present. We should develop research proposals that include stakeholders throughout the process, from the formulation of research questions to data collection and interpretation. The results of such studies can encourage new conversations between Dutch Caribbean people and between the Dutch Caribbean and the Kingdom of the Netherlands in order to stimulate positive social and political change.

REFERENCES

Allen, R. 2015. "Toward Reconstituting Caribbean Identity Discourse from within the Dutch Caribbean Island of Curacao." In *Caribbean Reasonings: Freedom, Power and Sovereignty, the Thought of Gordon K Lewis*, edited by Meeks, B. and J. McCalpin, 94-110: Ian Randle Publishers.

———. 2017. "Exploring Reality: Reflecting on Cultural Identities within a Localized Form of Cultural Studies on Curaçao." *'Whither the Caribbean': Stuart Hall's Intellectual Legacy Conference, June 1-3, Jamaica.*

Ansano, R. 2006. "René Römer: Between Striking a Path and Creating a Legacy." In: Allen, R. ed. *René Römer Als Inspirator: Actualisering Van Zijn Gedachtegoed*. Curacao: University of the Netherlands Antilles, pp. 9-15.

———. 2017. "What is Central to Curacao's History and National Identity? A Cultural Heritage Canon as a Tool for National Identity, Nation-Building and Nation-Branding." September 20-21, 2017.

Bales, K. 2004. *Disposable People: New Slavery in the Global Economy*. London: University of California Press.

Battle-Baptiste, W. 2011. *Black Feminist Archaeology*. Walnut Creek, California: Left Coast Press.

Blakey, M. and L. Rankin-Hill. 2009. *The New York African Burial Ground: Unearthing the African Presence in Colonial New York, Volume 1*. Washington DC: Howard University Press.

Broere, K. 2020. "De premier van Curaao: 'Op deze manier verzwakt Nederland onze positive." *De Volkskrant*, 1st July 2020.

Cain, A. 2015. "Slavery and Memory in the Netherlands: Who Needs Commemoration?" *Journal of African Diaspora Archaeology and Heritage* 4(3): 227-242.

Delle, J. and E. Clay 2019. *Archaeology of Domestic Landscapes of the Enslaved in the Caribbean*. Gainesville: University of Florida Press.

Eltis, D. and D. Richardson 2010. *Atlas of the Transatlantic Slave Trade*. London: Yale University Press.

Eyerman, R. 2001. *Cultural Trauma: Slavery and the Formation of African American Identity*. Cambridge: Cambridge University Press.

Franklin, M. 2004. *An Archaeological Study of the Rich Neck Slave Quarter and Enslaved Domestic Life*. Virginia: The Colonial Williamsburg Foundation.

Haar, H. 2017. "Haviser's Orange Movement Wants Constitutional Referendum." *St Maarten News*, 9th June 2017.

Haviser, J. 2001 "Historical Archaeology in the Netherlands Antilles and Aruba." In *Island Lives: Historical Archaeologies of the Caribbean*, edited by Farnsworth, P., 60-81. USA: University of Alabama Press.

Leslie, T. 2018. "Colonialism Begets Coloniality: A Case Study of Sint Eustatius, Dutch Caribbean." In *Smash the Pillars: Decoloniality and the Imaginary of Colour in the Dutch Kingdom*, edited by M. Weiner and A. Baez, 39-54. London: Lexington Books.

Marcha, V., P. Verweel, and J. Werkman. 2012. *Kleur Bekennen: Idealisering En Ontkenning Van De Eigen Huidskleur*. Amsterdam: Caribpublishing/BV Uitgeverij SWP.

Meade, N. 2018. "St Maarten is Still Striving to Recover from its Worst Hurricane in a Century." *The New Yorker*, 19th June 2018.

Nimako, K. and G. Willemsen. 2011. *The Dutch Atlantic: Slavery, Abolition and Emancipation*. London: Pluto Press.

Oostindie, G. 2005. *Paradise Overseas: The Dutch Caribbean: Colonialism and its Transatlantics Legacies*. Oxford: Macmillan Caribbean.

Oostindie, G. 2013. *Confronting Caribbean Challenges: Hybrid Identities and Governance in Small-Scale Island Jurisdictions*. Royal Netherlands Institute of Southeast Asian and Caribbean Studies (KITLV).

Patterson, O. 2012. "Trafficking, Gender and Slavery: Past and Present." In *The Legal Understanding of Slavery: From the Historical to the Contemporary*, edited by J. Allain, 322-359. Oxford: Oxford University Press.

Petitie24 2020. "Racisme moet verplicht behandeld worden op school." *Petitie24*. Accesses 8th July 2020. https://www.petitie24.nl/petitie/3098/racisme-moet-verplicht-behandeld-worden-op-school

Schneider, T. and K. Hayes 2020. "Epistemic colonialism: is it possible to decolonize archaeology?" *The American Indian Quarterly* 44(2): 127-148.

Smeulders, V. 2012. "Slavernij in Perspectief: Mondialisering En Erfgoed in Suriname, Ghana, Zuid-Afrika En Curacao."Erasmus Universiteit.

van der Ven, C. 2011. *Slagschaduwen: Erfenis Van Een Koloniaal Verleden*. Amsterdam: KIT Publishers.

Vissers, P. 2020. "Black Lives Matter NL: een losjes netwerk dat groeit en groeit." *Trouw*, 13th June 2020.

White, W. and C. Draycott 2020. "Why the Whiteness of Archaeology is a Problem." *Sapiens*, 7th July 2020.

Glossary

Bomba	Slave driver (Papiamentu)
Brua	African-influenced belief system in Curaçao (seen as negative, witchcraft)
CUR	Airport code for the Hato International Airport, Curaçao
EUX	Airport code for the FD Roosevelt Airport, St Eustatius
Fitó	Overseer (Papiamentu)
Inrap	*Institut national de recherches archéologiques préventives* (French National Institute for Archaeological Rescue Research)
LSAMAT	Lingual surface attrition of the maxillary anterior teeth
Mondi	Countryside/Curaçaoan bush (Papiamentu)
Montamentu	African-influenced belief system in Curaçao (seen as positive, ancestors)
NAAM	National Archaeological Anthropological Memory Management, Curaçao
Obeah	African-influenced belief system practised mainly on English-speaking Caribbean islands
SECAR	St Eustatius Centre for Archaeological Research
Shon	Master (Papiamentu)
SIMARC	St Maarten Archaeological Center
Statia	Affectionate name for St Eustatius
St Maarten	Dutch (southern) side of the island of St Maarten/St Martin/SXM
St Martin	French (northern) side of the island of St Maarten/St Martin/SXM
SXM	Airport code for the Princess Juliana International Airport, often used to refer to the island as a whole
Tambú	Dance performed in Curaçao; accompanied by singing which often forms political commentary; and the *tambú* drum (Papiamentu)
White guilt	The guilt felt by white people who see their racial group as having unearned advantages over those of other races
WIC	*West-Indische Compagnie* (Dutch West India Company)

Index

A
Agriculture 30, 31, 72, 75, 92
Alcohol 36, 74, 88, 95-96
Amulet...........................28, 62, 70, 100, 102
Ancestry ...1, 9, 17, 20, 33, 38, 41, 43, 58-60, 104

B
Bare life   40
Black Harry............................... 63, 64
Bonaire 2, 3, 6, 7, 117
Brua 28

C
Catholicism 16, 18, 25-28, 38, 61, 63, 76,
Christianity 3, 62, 63, 65, 75, 88, 102, 104
Code Noir 14, 93, 95
Coping mechanisms...... 18, 36, 37, 74, 97, 99

D
Dance 28, 36, 37, 42, 78, 97, 98, 117
Dental modification 88, 89, 104
DNA 89
Domestic labour 16, 20, 21, 33, 41, 57, 60, 74, 92, 105

E
Emic.. 6, 116
Emotion 1, 7, 8
Escape 37, 38, 57, 58, 71-73, 94, 106, 107
Etic 6, 116
Eurocentric 4, 7, 9

F
Family......... 6, 9, 21, 27, 34, 38, 54, 79, 98, 101, 105
Feminism 5, 116
Food17, 22-24, 31, 33-35, 42, 57, 66, 69, 71, 86, 93, 95, 98, 102, 105, 106, 110
Frederick Douglass 40
Free port 54

French 2, 4, 14, 19, 55, 58, 60, 61, 71, 74, 87, 88, 90, 93, 95, 98, 102, 105, 106, 108, 109

G
Games..78, 96, 97
Griot 98
Guene..37, 98

H
Hermeneutics 2, 6
Homespace 24, 25, 71, 96
Hurricane...................... 58, 90, 93, 105, 117

I
Indigenous 24, 31, 38, 41, 42, 43, 59, 60, 66, 87, 94, 97, 102
Interdisciplinarity 2, 5, 7, 116, 118
Intersectionality.. 5, 7
Isotopic analysis.................. 20, 34, 89, 104

J
Jollification   99

K
Knip 25, 29, 30, 35

L
Labour..16, 19, 20-22, 29, 30, 34, 40- 42, 60, 87, 93, 109, 118
Leeward Islands 2, 3
Leprosy..76, 77, 79
Lingual surface attrition
of the maxillary anterior
teeth...............42, 60, 104, 105
Literacy..38, 57
Looting   68

M
Macroscale   8
Manumission 26, 27, 33, 38, 56, 66, 93
Marriage... 17, 28, 69, 70

125

Medicine.. 8, 24, 62, 100
Men............................ 2, 20, 27, 34, 66, 68, 98
Methodism 61, 63, 64, 102, 108
Microscale   8
'Mild' slavery..................4, 15, 20, 109, 115
Modern slavery 118
Montamentu   28
Music..................................36, 37, 78, 98, 107

N
Nanzi 36, 37
Netherlands Antilles....................................2, 4

O
Obeah.......................61-64, 68, 100-104
Olaudah Equiano....................................... 56, 74
Osteobiography   8

P
Paga tera 29, 40-43
Panopticon 30, 39, 55
Papiamentu 3, 4, 7, 16, 18, 24, 25, 28, 30, 31, 37, 41, 42
Postcolonial theory.......5-7, 9, 30, 40, 116
Poison..................................... 24, 59, 100-102
Psychological effects ..2, 9, 16, 18, 20-22, 24, 36, 37, 41, 54, 57, 69, 70, 74, 89, 97, 107-109, 115-117
Punishment 14-16, 21, 22, 41, 73, 74, 89, 101, 107, 108

Q
Quakers   102

R
Reburial   77
Reflexivity..6, 9
Resistance...18, 25, 36-40, 57, 71, 87, 98, 100, 105, 108, 110, 116, 117

S
Sailor............................... 31, 34, 56, 60, 66
Salt 3, 15, 20, 37, 71, 86, 87, 90, 93, 95, 97, 107, 108, 117
Scurvy...........................22, 33, 65, 66, 71
Shoes   30
Slave trade 1, 19, 20, 58, 60, 74, 93
Smoking.................................... 77, 78, 97, 103

Spanish ...4, 19, 25, 39, 41, 43, 58, 61, 87, 110
Storytelling ..23, 37, 36, 92, 97, 100, 101, 105-107
Stress 18, 20-22, 31, 34, 57, 65
Subaltern 5, 9
Sugar 20, 33, 38, 42, 43, 54, 56, 64, 65, 72, 87, 90, 92, 93, 95, 96, 99, 104, 110, 115
Syncretism 24, 56, 66, 77, 78, 94, 97, 102, 116

T
Tambú 28, 37, 97
Tourist....................................... 68, 86, 90, 110
Trees 15, 30, 31, 54, 59, 63, 74, 96, 97, 101, 102, 107
Triangulation 7, 8
Trinta di mei..30, 117
Tula... 25, 30, 37, 117

V
Venezuela 2, 25, 26, 38, 39, 117

W
Walls 18, 24, 29, 90-92
Water....15, 18, 20, 21, 28, 36, 72, 74, 87, 88, 92, 94, 97, 102
West Africa 19, 22, 24, 28, 36, 62, 68, 74, 75, 89, 97, 98, 105
White guilt   1
Windward Islands 2, 3, 110
Women..1, 6, 7, 16, 18-23, 27, 60, 67, 68, 69, 92, 98, 100, 102, 105, 107

Y
Yard sweeping................................24, 66, 67

www.ingramcontent.com/pod-product-compliance
Lightning Source LLC
Chambersburg PA
CBHW062027290426
44108CB00025B/2806